W9-BSB-877

the complete vegetable book

the complete vegetable book

Clare Connery

photography by Sandra Lane

BARNES
&NOBLE
BOOKS
NEW YORK

To my daughter, Clare — for health and happiness

Publishing Director: Laura Bamford

Project Manager: Jeni Wright
Editor: Katey Day

Creative Director: Keith Martin
Senior Designer: Geoff Fennell

Photographer: Sandra Lane
Home Economist: Oona van den Berg
Stylist: Mary Norden
Picture Researcher: Wendy Gay

Indexer: Hilary Bird

Senior Production Controller: Bonnie Ashby

The Complete Vegetable Book

First Published in Great Britain in 1998 by
Hamlyn
an imprint of Reed Consumer Books Limited
Michelin House, 81 Fulham Road,
London, SW3 6RB

This edition published by Barnes & Noble, Inc.,
by arrangement with Hamlyn.

1998 Barnes & Noble Books

M 10 9 8 7 6 5 4 3 2 1

ISBN 0 7607 1156 9

Design, text, and illustrations copyright © 1998
Reed Consumer Books Limited

Printed and Bound in China

contents

Not for me a childhood in which the image of vegetables was blighted by the odor of overcooked greens in a steamy kitchen. I had a green-fingered grandmother who had gotten her household budgeting to a fine art, walked everywhere, and revered her small kitchen garden. My happiest childhood times were spent in her company in her little wooden cottage by the sea. Sitting at her tiny kitchen table, or on the kitchen steps surveying her vegetable patch, it was always a pleasure to eat up my greens. My adventurous granny introduced me to the avocado and the eggplant, to kohlrabi, and celery root, and it was with her that I went on my first mushroom hunt.

For my grandmother, food was the greatest pleasure, her homegrown vegetables were a special daily treat. For me, food has been the focal point of my working life, the way in which I have earned my living, but I have never lost that initial fascination with growing things of all colors, shapes, sizes, and flavors, implanted by Granny Smyth. I was extremely fortunate to have had such a wonderful educational "supplement."

Today we live in a highly automated, ready-prepared, pre-packaged, just-heat-and-serve society. Basic knowledge about food, what it is, how it grows, what goodness it contains, how to prepare it efficiently and hygienically, by-passes many children altogether. The standard of teaching of such things in schools is variable, to say the least. If all schools provided information about the nutritional benefits and sheer tasty delight of a different vegetable every week, then I believe we would have a healthier society. But, I must get off my soapbox!

One never stops hearing about food. Hardly a week goes by but we read about the nutritional benefits of some vegetable or other, all those vitamins, minerals, and trace elements, the newly discovered protection against some disease or other. The preparation for this book not only involved me in learning about these nutritional attributes but also in studying the history and geographical origins of each vegetable. In addition, of course, I immersed myself in the creation and testing of all the recipes. What an illuminating story can be told about vegetables, and how fascinating it is to follow their progress through history.

I was transported to ancient origins in the Andean foothills and Asia Minor, visited the tables of the Aztecs and the Egyptians, and learned about the health-giving properties of vegetables known to the Greeks and Romans. So, with the aid of modern scientific and medical analysis, we are really learning about nutritional benefits already known many centuries ago.

Styles of cooking come and go, but we are fortunate in that the variety of ingredients available to us now is unprecedented in history. Not only has horticulture progressed so that natural seasons can be extended, but easy transportation means that vegetables from all over the United States, and even beyond, reach our stores in tip-top condition throughout the year. For me, this book has been a true labor of love, the seeds of inspiration for which were planted all those years ago in that wooden cottage by the sea. How appropriate that I should be writing these words by the window in a summerhouse just above the little harbor in County Down, Northern Ireland, with the lingering memory of that late summer and early fall long ago.

introduction

The book presents portraits of over sixty different vegetables from all over the world, from the essential onion to decorative mizuna greens, grouped into sections. First there are Leafy Greens & Brassicas, which include those several types of crisp and delicious oriental greens which are relatively new to the supermarket shelves. Next come Stalks & Stems (far more interesting than the name implies), including the aristocratic asparagus and the dramatic globe artichoke, which looks so imposing when growing in the garden. The Onion Family, flavor enhancers and medicinal marvels through the centuries, come next, then Roots & Tubers, from the potato and its carbohydrate rivals from around the world (the taro and the yucca), to the radishes essential in the diet of the workers who built the pyramids, and the Jerusalem artichoke, whose identity in soups always mystifies my dinner guests. Podded Vegetables — from the ancient pea and bean to the New World corn and the mucilaginous okra — follow, then the gloriously colored Fruiting Vegetables, including the family of peppers and chilies, the squashes, which bring brightness as the days draw in toward winter, and the eggplant. Finally, though not strictly vegetables at all, but so important for flavor and texture, come Mushrooms, wild and cultivated, mass-produced and plentiful, or fickle and hidden in jealously guarded secret locations.

No one can entirely deny their origins, however widely traveled he or she may be. This selection of recipes chosen to illustrate these vegetables reflects my own wanderings through life, linking the traditional with the very modern, the rustic with the sophisticated. There are some timeless recipes like Rustic Greek Salad, then there are those which owe much to the growing popularity of exotic cuisines such as Wilted Greens with Water Chestnuts & Black Bean Sauce. I am not a vegetarian and this book is deliberately written so as not to exclude meat eaters. It is rather a celebration of the central role that vegetables should play in our everyday diet. Not only because of their nutritional value, but because of the variety of flavors they offer. There are dishes intended for all occasions, from quick snacks and light lunches to informal suppers and stylish entertaining. They also reflect our increasingly cosmopolitan tastes. I believe that this selection of recipes has something to offer all age groups, and certainly there is nothing here which my intrepid grandmother or my very modern daughter could not have sat at the same table and enjoyed.

For convenience, the recipes are divided conventionally into soups, appetizers and entrées. The entrée category has been further divided into cooking methods — Stews; Stir-fries, Pan-fries & Broils, and Roasts & Bakes. In addition I have included some Sauces & Dressings, and a selection of Dips & Salsas, so important for modern entertaining. Finally, there are the Side-dishes, a selection of breads, scones, chips, and other tidbits to eat with vegetable dishes. Everything one could want in a vegetable book and all beautifully illustrated with evocative photographs.

I hope you will enjoy my selection and be inspired not only to try the recipes but also to experiment to create many others for yourself.

Clare Connery
Strangford, 1998

directory

leafy greens & brassicas

Swiss chard

Beta vulgaris

This leafy vegetable is rich in vitamins A and C, and also contains some vitamin B and the minerals, sodium, potassium, and iron.

Also called silverbeet, silver chard, and seakale beet, why this vegetable is commonly known as Swiss chard is something of a mystery. What is known is that it can be traced back to the ancient Greeks, and that the Romans introduced it to central and northern Europe and from there to Persia and China. In its wild form, it can be found all around the Mediterranean and British coasts.

Swiss chard is from the same family as red beet, but it is grown for its leaves rather than its roots. It comes in two varieties, the technicolor red or ruby chard (also called rhubarb chard), and the more familiar white variety, which has broad white leaf stalks and midribs supporting glossy green fleshy leaves. Both the stalks and leaves can be eaten. The stalks are succulent and juicy, not unlike celery. The leaves are similar in taste to spinach and are often substituted for it, although chard leaves are larger, more fleshy and substantial. Chard has one particular advantage over spinach in that it contains less oxalic acid, which means that its iron content can be more readily absorbed by our bodies.

When buying chard, look for shiny, crisp, brightly-colored leaves and crisp spines. It is often sold in heads rather than leaves, and these should be firm and tightly packed. Because the stalks and leaves are different in texture and thickness, separate them before cooking by cutting round the central rib of the stalk which runs up into the leaf (use kitchen scissors.) Wash the stalks and leaves well, then spin or shake the leaves dry. Either shred the leaves and cook them as you would spinach or cabbage, or leave them whole to be blanched and stuffed with rice, beans, or other vegetables. Cut the stalks and central spine into 2–4 inch lengths about ½ inch wide, stripping off any stringy parts, then cook them until tender in boiling water to which a little lemon juice has been added. Serve the cooked Swiss chard with melted butter, or with a cream, white, or tomato sauce. Swiss chard is also a popular ingredient in stir-fries.

Chinese mustard greens

Brassica juncea

These are a good source of vitamins C and D and the B group. They are high in calcium, iron, and potassium.

These are thought to have originated in Central Asia and grow wild throughout the Mediterranean. For flavor, they are certainly the most interesting of the oriental greens and in no way bland – on the contrary, they are hot and spicy with a strong mustard taste, as the name suggests. In Europe they are grown solely for their mustard seeds, in India and Asia for their seed oil, but in China they have been developed for their leaves as well. Look for them in the oriental vegetable sections of large supermarkets and in oriental shops, where they are called gai choy and sometimes described as mustard cabbage.

In appearance mustard greens are not unlike spring greens, slightly elongated in shape, with loose, almost puckered leaves in varying shades of green, from light lime to deep bottle green with a purple tinge. The leaves are coarse in texture and are best cooked like spring greens – shredded then boiled or steamed, with any coarse stalks removed. They can also be cooked quickly in a wok, which is the way I favor, either torn into pieces or shredded, and served with a light Chinese dressing or sauce.

If you grow your own, the seedlings or small young leaves can be eaten raw and are delicious in salads. I just love to pick and nibble every time I pass a plant.

Older leaves are more pungent than young leaves, but they lose some of their fire when cooked.

kale

Brassica oleracea

Acephala group

A good source of calcium, iron and vitamins A, E, and C.

We in Ireland have a strong affinity with this hardy vegetable, mainly because of its partnership with potato in the preparation of colcannon, one of Ireland's national dishes. Of the two vegetables, the potato may be the better known, but kale has a much longer European pedigree. It is aptly described as a sort of primitive cabbage, thick stalked and loose-léaved, no doubt closer in appearance to the brassicas known to the Greeks and Romans than to the hard-hearted and headed cabbages we know today. Wild or sea cabbage, its wild ancestor, is still found here and there along the coasts of western Europe, although it is not always certain whether these plants are truly wild or are simply escapes from cultivation which have reverted to their original form.

Curly kale Also known as cottage kale, curled kale, German kale, true kale and borecole (the anglicized version of the Dutch word *Boerenkool*, meaning peasant's cabbage), this is the most commonly available kale, although even then it is not always easy to find. Other names for it include Scotch kale, for this enormously robust and hardy vegetable which thrives on frost and snow, was once a staple in Scotland, where vegetable gardens in the Lowlands were formerly known as kale-yards or kailyards. Kail brose was peasant food in Scotland, a soup made by boiling an ox head or cow heel and then stirring cooked kale and a large handful of oatmeal into the cooking liquid. Green or pan kale was a meatless variation of this dish which was eaten during Lent. Kailkenny is a similar dish to colcannon and is found in northern Scotland.

Available all year, curly kale is probably the strongest tasting of all the brassicas. It has attractive frilled, curly leaves which grow from a coarse central stalk. In some varieties the leaves are crimped rather like parsley, or even serrated like small palm leaves. The color is a dark, luscious green. Some curly kale plants can grow to over 3 feet high, giving the effect of being almost tree like. As a result, gardeners often use kale for foliage in borders. Indeed, some curly kale stems become so thick and straight that they are dried and made into canes.

Collards or collard greens These are milder in taste with smooth leaves, thinner than those of true kale, and without the frilly or crimped edges. Although they were originally used in the 18th century as a winter feed for cattle, today collards have become a popular vegetable and are frequently used in stews and *étouffée* dishes in the Deep South.

Purple or silver kale This is an ornamental variety, grown almost exclusively for display, and is especially popular with Japanese gardeners.

When buying kale, look for heads with crisp leaves, vibrant color and stiff and firm stalks. As with all leafy vegetables, check for obvious signs of age, discoloration, bruising and limpness. Leaves should be crisp, their color vibrant and the stalk stiff and firm. Kale is a robust leafy vegetable, so when bought fresh and in good condition, it should keep well for several days in a cool place or in a plastic bag in the refrigerator. Simplicity is the essence in both preparation and cooking. Remove any leaves you don't like the look or feel of, then break those remaining from the stalk, cutting out any thick stalky spines from the leaves. Wash the leaves (discard the stalks), drain well and either leave whole, tear into pieces or roll into a cigar shape and shred.

Boil in no more than 1 inch of water for 3–5 minutes, then drain, return to the pan, season with salt and pepper, and finish with melted butter. Another method is to toss the kale in bacon fat after boiling and serve with fried bacon and mashed potatoes — an Irish speciality. Boiled and served slightly crisp, kale is excellent with fried fish. In contrast, when combined with mashed potatoes to make colcannon, it needs to be very well cooked so that it can be easily mashed with the potatoes to produce a speckled green mass. Because of its robust taste and texture, kale combines well with strong hot spices.

cauliflower

Brassica oleracea

Botrytis group

A rich source of vitamins A and C, folic acid, phosphorus, sulfur, calcium and sodium.

The cauliflower's early progress from its ancient Middle Eastern origins as a sort of spindly cabbage with a small flower head are a little obscure, but what we do know is that the resourceful Moors introduced it to Spain in the early Middle Ages, and that it has grown on the island of Cyprus with great success for many centuries. Cauliflower was certainly grown widely in Europe and Britain in the 17th century, and the description "coleflower" or "cabbage flower" dates from this time.

The cauliflower is a close cousin of broccoli, but it is distinctive enough to have its own name – *Botrytis*, from the Greek word for a bunch of grapes, because of the obvious similarity. In addition to the familiar large white and dwarf varieties, other cauliflowers vary in color from snowy white through lime green to purple. Romanesco is one of several varieties seen in specialist grocers. It looks like a cross between broccoli and cauliflower and has very pretty, textured heads. The taste of Romanesco is similar to cauliflower and the color can be white or pale green.

Believe your own eyes when choosing cauliflower, because freshness really does stand out. When in tip-top condition, the head should be tightly packed with a mass of creamy white curds swathed in crisp green leaves. Above all, it should look and smell fresh and beautiful.

Trim off any coarse bottom leaves and the woody base of the stalk. Very large cauliflowers are best cut into halves, quarters, or broken into flowerets. The tender leaves can be left on or trimmed off and steamed or boiled as a separate vegetable. When I break cauliflower into flowerets I try to leave a little stalk attached to each one or group of curds. This I peel with a vegetable peeler to ensure that it cooks in the same time as the head.

I generally steam whole cauliflower or flowerets until just tender. When it is whole, test it after 10 minutes: it should feel tender but still have plenty of bite. If you prefer to boil cauliflower, use only a small amount of water and time in the same way. Whole cauliflower is good coated with a rich cheese sauce and browned under the broiler, either as a main dish with crusty bread or as an accompaniment to roast beef or lamb.

Cauliflower is also good broken into bite-sized pieces and stir-fried in a little hot oil with chili and cumin, either on its own or with other crisp vegetables. Before stir-frying it is best par-boiled for 1 minute, refreshed until cold, then drained and dried. Bite-sized flowerets can also be included in stews and stir-fries and any leftover raw flowerets can be used to make to make a creamy cauliflower soup. For this I use small flowerets and leave them whole rather than puréeing. More often than not, I snap the head into bite-sized pieces and eat them raw with creamy yogurt. You can also serve them as part of a raw vegetable platter with dips, or include them in a cold salad.

Cabbage is a rich source of vitamins A, B, C, D and E, and a good source of iron, potassium and calcium.

One smell inextricably linked with my schooldays is that of cabbage and floor polish, somehow united and suspended above a damp and dismal dining hall — the result of the execution of the cabbage by drowning in gallons of boiling water. Fortunately, I made no connection between that colorless watery mass and the crisp green delicacy, topped with a knob of country butter, which was grown and presented with love and understanding by my mother and grandmother.

It would appear that the earliest type of cabbage was a wild loose-leaved plant, prevalent around the coasts of Europe. The modern-day equivalent still grows in coastal regions of France and Italy, a tall, thick-stemmed variety. Both the ancient Greeks and the Romans held it in high esteem, and it is believed that the Celts, originating themselves in central Europe, were the first to grow "headed" cabbage – the word "brassica" is derived from the Celtic word *bresic* meaning cabbage. By medieval times these round tight-headed cabbages were an important part of the diet of the poor, and by the 16th century the crinkled-leaf Savoy was becoming established in Europe.

cabbage
Brassica oleracea
Capitata group

Freshness is all when buying cabbage. A hearted cabbage should feel substantial and heavy. To prepare, remove the outer leaves where necessary. If the cabbage is loose-leaved, cut off as many leaves as required, removing the core. Store the rest in a bag in the refrigerator for future use. Rinse well under cold running water, shake dry, then place the leaves on top of each other in a pile. Roll up like a cigar and shred finely (opposite page.) If the cabbage is tight-headed, cut it into quarters and cut out the tough stalk before shredding finely, then wash and drain. If the leaves are to be stuffed, leave them whole.

To cook shredded cabbage, put it into a large saucepan with a teaspoon of butter and just enough water to prevent burning. Cover and cook over a high heat for a few minutes until just tender, shaking the pan and turning the cabbage occasionally. Drain and serve immediately, with lots of freshly ground black pepper and more butter. Take care not to overcook cabbage as this will cause it to lose much of its nutritional value. Shredded cabbage can also be steamed, and is excellent stir-fried, on its own or with other vegetables.

Only when blanching (part-cooking) whole leaves for stuffing should you use a large pan full of boiling water. Drop the leaves in for just long enough to make them pliable enough to be rolled.

Heavy-headed winter cabbage can be cooked, whole or quartered, in lots of boiling water, or along with boiled beef, bacon or ham (this is one of the traditional ways of cooking cabbage in Ireland.) Winter cabbage can also be shredded, when it lends itself to long, slow cooking in stews and soups as well as braised dishes. It adds texture to stir-fried dishes, as does red cabbage, which is well suited to these cooking methods, as well as pickling.

Cabbages belong to the brassica clan of vegetables, and there are many varieties. However, all cabbages contain the sulfur compounds which are responsible for the famous smell given off by overcooked cabbage.

Red cabbage Wonderful to look at, this purple-headed cabbage is crisp and crunchy when raw or pickled, but needs long, slow cooking. It is ideal stewed or braised, particularly with apples, vine fruits, honey, and red wine.

Savoy cabbage (opposite page) This handsome cabbage has deep green crinkly leaves that are tender and require little cooking. It is highly versatile, good boiled, steamed or braised. The head can be cooked whole, or the large leaves used for stuffing. As the leaves are crisp and delicate in flavor, they are excellent raw in salads.

Spring greens With their vibrant colors and delicate loose leaves, these are something to look forward to after the hard tight heads of winter. They often have slightly pointed heads and little or no heart because it is usual to eat them when they are still young.

White or Dutch cabbage With its hard round head, this cold weather cabbage is composed of silky, creamy white to pale green leaves packed tightly together. Its crisp texture makes it perfect for raw salads, particularly coleslaw. It can also be boiled, steamed and braised, but it lacks some of the depth of flavor of its leafy green relatives.

Brussels sprouts

Brassica oleracea

Gemmifera group

Brussels sprouts are an excellent source of vitamins C, A, and E, as well as potassium and iron.

As inventions go, the Brussels sprout is one of the most remarkable. Take a cabbage, cut off the head and develop the stem so that nine cabbages sprout like rosebuds along its length. Ingenious.

To the cook, there is only one variety, whose dark green tightly packed heads appear in the shops from late summer into winter (though purists say they are not worth eating until they have experienced the first frosts). Better known to gardener-cooks is a magnificent red variety, which not only tastes good but also makes an excellent ornamental border plant.

The maxim "small is beautiful" certainly applies to sprouts. Here the German word *Rosenkohl* does the little wonders justice. If sprouts were treated more like delicate rosebuds, the end result would be more satisfying more often. When they are at their freshest, all compact greenness and with a minimum amount of cooking, their nutty flavor is a delight.

Choose small, tightly packed, bright green sprouts. Try to avoid really large sprouts — my rule is a maximum of 1 inch: any larger and you run the risk of coarse texture and flavor. It is best to cook them within a couple of days of purchase.

All you need to do before cooking is to trim off the outer leaves along with a sliver from the stalky base, then give the sprouts a quick wash. If the leaves are loose and there is a risk of insects inside, soak the sprouts in cold salted water for about 15 minutes, then rinse well. Make a small cross in the stalk end and either cook them in a large saucepan of fast-boiling water to cover, for a maximum of 5 minutes until just tender, or steam for 3–5 minutes. Sprouts get soft and squashy, lose their color and develop a rank smell if overcooked. After draining, toss them in butter and salt and freshly ground black pepper before serving. At Christmas it is traditional to toss them with chestnuts, on other occasions you can substitute slivers of toasted almonds or whole roasted hazelnuts for chestnuts. As an accompaniment to game, top them with crisp and golden butter-fried bread crumbs.

Alternatively, stir-fry sprouts, either halved, quartered or sliced, or serve them raw, left whole if small or cut in half. Raw sprouts are also good in salads, whole, halved, quartered, shredded, sliced, or grated. This way there is little loss of vitamins, minerals, taste, or texture.

High in vitamin A, with significant amounts of vitamin C, folic acid, and iron, broccoli also has moderate levels of calcium.

Originating in ancient Asia Minor and the Eastern Mediterranean, broccoli in its sprouting form seems to have been popular with the Romans – the word broccoli comes from *brocco*, the Italian for sprout or shoot.

Sprouting broccoli has a mass of delicate flower heads loosely arranged at the top of long slender stalks. The color ranges from white (not often found) through green to blue-green and the original dusky purple, which turns green when cooked. Chinese sprouting broccoli, also called Chinese kale, looks like sprouting broccoli, but is more spindly, with looser yellow or white flowerets. Calabrese is an Italian creation of the late Middle Ages. It takes its name from Calabria, where it was developed. It is what most people today consider as broccoli, often sold wrapped in plastic. It has a large heavy head of blue-green flower buds on a chunky stalk.

Broccoli stalks should be firm and crisp and the leaves vigorous. Sprouting broccoli has a shorter shelf life than calabrese, so should be used within 1–2 days. Trim the ends of sprouting broccoli, cut off any tough or damaged stalks, then remove any bruised or wilted leaves. Rinse in cold running water then peel the stalk from below the

broccoli
Brassica oleracea
Italica group

flower head to the end. This allows the stalk and delicate head to cook in the same time. For calabrese, cut the head into even-sized flowerets, each with a section of stalk, which should be peeled.

Steam the stalks of sprouting broccoli for 3–5 minutes until just tender. Alternatively, lay them in a large deep skillet, cover with boiling water and boil quickly until tender. Cook calabrese in boiling water for the same length of time. Broccoli and calabrese respond well to stir-frying. To prevent the flowerets burning before the stalks cook, remove the heads from the stalks and add these to the pan when the stalks are almost cooked. Broccoli requires little embellishment other than melted butter and freshly ground black pepper, but it is also delicious with lemon butter or grated Parmesan cheese, or with a cheese hollandaise or béarnaise sauce. It can be used in gratins, stews, stir-fries, or soups, and in raw vegetable platters.

they "bolt" or develop flowers, lends them to be grown along paths, in herbaceous borders, or in tubs and pots. Like the more familiar salad leaves and spring greens, they are also grown as "cut and come again" vegetables. Bok choy, also called bok-choi and pak-choi, comes in many varieties, the smallest being no more than 3–4 inches high. In some varieties its stalky base is reminiscent of celery, hence its alternative name of Chinese celery cabbage, but its leaves are smoother and more glossy, spoon-like in shape, and a deep rich green in color. The creamy white midrib and leaf stems are striking in contrast. Each plant is joined at the base of the thick stem by a small root which holds the leaves together.

A good source of vitamins C and D and the B group, with a high content of calcium, iron, and potassium.

There really isn't anything exotic about oriental vegetables, particularly brassicas like bok choy (pak-choi) and Chinese (Napa) cabbage (page 27), supermarkets now stock a wide range. They are also in the gourmet gardener's repertoire, since they are fairly easy to grow, even in the smallest of spaces. Their attractive appearance, both before and after

Bok choy is a delicate plant and consequently does not keep long. When buying, look for plants with fresh green leaves. The stems should be crisp and bright. Pay attention to the smell: it should be fresh. Check the heads of bok choy at home, remove any damaged or less than fresh leaves. Put the head in an open container, cover lightly with wax paper or foil, and place in the salad drawer of the refrigerator; it should keep fresh for several days.

When bok choy is young, small and tender, it can be eaten raw as a salad leaf. It is slightly peppery in taste, with more flavor than Chinese cabbage.

Bigger plants can be prepared and cooked like Swiss chard. The thick stems, which are juicy and sweet, can be boiled or steamed and served with butter, an oil dressing or a sweet and sour sauce. The leaves can be torn or shredded and lightly boiled in the minimum of water, like spinach or other delicate leafy greens. Alternatively, the leaves and stems can be sliced and braised together as in chow mein, or stir-fried in a fragrant oil and dressed with a flavorsome sauce or seasoning.

bok choy
Brassica rapa Sinensis

mizuna greens

Brassica rapa nipposinica

This Japanese brassica is a good source of vitamins C and D and the B group. It is also valued for its calcium, iron and potassium content. These are a particularly attractive variety of oriental greens, loved as much for their delicate spiky fronds as for their mild peppery flavor. Although originally from China, it is the Japanese who use them most frequently in their cooking. They are a handsome vegetable with finely divided and glossy deep green leaves on slender white stalks. They are especially decorative in the garden, either lining the edges of a path or creating an attractive display in a herbaceous border. They grow in loose bushy clumps, which can reach a height of about 9 inches.

A relative of parsley and coriander, mizuna greens are only just finding their way into the shops, so it is best to sow your own for a guaranteed supply.

Before using, pick the greens over carefully and wash them under cold running water. Spin-dry like other salad leaves and store in a container in the bottom of the refrigerator. Use as quickly as possible.

The leaves are perfect in salads when small and young. As they get older, they can be stir-fried with other leafy greens. Mizuna greens can also be used as a garnish for oriental dishes.

Chinese cabbage

Brassica rapa Pekinensis

Chinese cabbage contains moderate levels of vitamins A, B, C, and D, with folic acid, potassium, and calcium.

This is the best known of the oriental brassicas, also confusingly called Napa cabbage, Chinese leaves, pe-tsai, Peking cabbage, wong-bok, Shantung cabbage, and celery cabbage. It is assumed that its history in China is ancient, although the first written record is from the 5th century AD — recent in terms of Chinese history.

It looks like a substantial chunky lettuce, a huge head of celery or a form of Cos lettuce, but it is much more leafy and substantial, weighing anything from 2–4 pounds. The leaves are slightly crinkly in texture, striped with long, wide, smooth white ribs fanning out towards frilled edges. It has a pleasant crunchy texture and the robust leaves are excellent in leafy salads. In taste they are reminiscent of celery and cabbage put together.

There are two other types of Chinese cabbage available. The round-hearted or barrel-shaped variety is more like conventional cabbage, with wrinkly leaves tightly wrapped around a dense heart. The loose-headed variety has more textured leaves, fluffy tops and a cream-colored center.

Chinese cabbage should look fresh and lively, be well filled out, and feel heavy and substantial. When bought in its prime, it will keep for several weeks in a plastic bag in the bottom of the refrigerator; if stored in a cool and dark, dry place, it will keep for several months. Don't wash it before it is needed.

To prepare, take off the coarse outer leaves, then use the rest. For a salad, I slice the whole head finely across the leaves. Or I cut away the spine and stalk and cut them into fine sticks for contrasting textures, then tear the large leaves into pieces and shred the heart. When used raw in salad, Chinese cabbage is best combined with other salad leaves, like arugula and chicory, which are more powerful in flavor, and tossed in a well-flavored dressing.

To cook, cut the spines or stalks out of the leaves and cut them into pieces, then boil or steam. Serve with a light creamy sauce, or toss in butter or oil and season with salt and pepper. In oriental cooking, shredded leaves are most often stir-fried or tossed in a light sesame oil flavored with garlic, chili powder, and ginger. A little sugar can be added, or a dash of rice wine or dry sherry, with a little chili powder, oyster sauce, or black bean sauce.

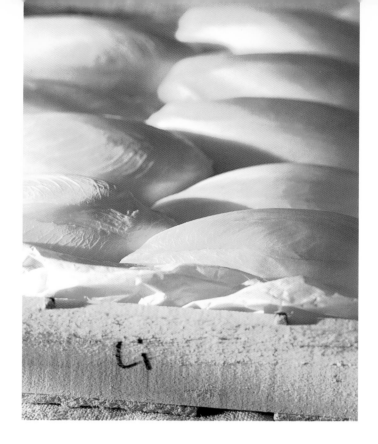

endive
Cichorium intybus

A good source of vitamins A and C, calcium, potassium, and phosphorus, endive is low in calories.

I first encountered Belgian endive or witloof as a student in London many years ago. I was fascinated by the tight, uniformly shaped heads, wrapped in bright blue paper to preserve their pale color, laid out in rows in shallow boxes.

Chicory had been grown in Europe for hundreds of years, so that the root could be roasted, ground, and added to coffee. However, blanched chicory, known as endive, was discovered by chance when, in the middle of the last century, a Monsieur Bezier of the Brussels Botanical Gardens, wanting a supply of chicory for his coffee in the winter, removed some roots from his salad bed, cut off most of the foliage, and planted the roots in a darkened shed. The result: small compact shoots of tightly furled leaves without the bitterness normally associated with chicory. Monsieur Bezier kept his discovery secret and it was only after his death that his wife passed on details of the process. This blanched form of chicory became big business in Belgium, hence its name of Belgian endive. Witloof, meaning "white leaf," is the Flemish name.

There is also a red form of endive, the same as the white except for the pigmentation on the leaf tips. As a decorative addition to the salad bowl it is very pretty, but the color runs as soon as it is subjected to heat.

Radicchio is red, unforced chicory or endive that grows green until exposed to cold weather. It is petite and round rather like a small cabbage, with wine-red leaves and cream ribs (opposite page). Its flavor is very distinctive like endive, with a pleasant, slightly bitter edge.

The third variety of endive, also unforced and perhaps less well known, is sugarloaf. It looks quite like a romaine lettuce, but with a noticeable "back of the tongue" flavor to the crisp green leaves.

When in prime condition, all forms of endive should have firm, tightly furled leaves. The witloof chicory should taper to a neat point and not look as if it is about to burst into flower. Choose even-sized heads, preferably individually wrapped if you can find them. If not, wrap them in brown paper as soon as you get them home and store them in the bottom of the refrigerator, where they should keep for 4–5 days.

To prepare endive, remove any damaged leaves and

trim the root end, cutting off any discolored parts. Wash under cold running water and pat dry. If using the endive raw in a salad, remove individual leaves, and toss with a light fruit-flavored vinaigrette, or combine with segments of citrus fruit or other sweet firm fruits such as apple or pear. The whole leaves are also good eaten raw, perfect for dipping in sauces or guacamole. Alternatively, keep the chicory heads intact and cut into diagonal ¼ inch slices, then toss with other leaves or salad ingredients such as celery, walnuts, ham, cold chicken, and sharp cheese.

Cooking changes the nature of endive, intensifying its flavor and bitterness, but never so much that it makes it unpleasant. Heat also changes its color and texture, and it can look rather unattractive unless browned slightly in butter after boiling or steaming, or covered with a sauce, dressing or garnish.

When preparing endive heads for cooking, it is received wisdom to whittle out a small cone from the core of the vegetable. This is said to reduce bitterness, but I am not altogether convinced, so experiment for yourself.

To boil endive, drop the heads into a large saucepan of fast boiling water to which the juice of ½–1 lemon has been added. This helps to retain its color. During cooking, push the endive heads under the water with a spoon as they tend to rise and float. Boil for 4–5 minutes until just tender, then drain well and squeeze the heads carefully between your hands to remove the very last drop of unwanted liquid. Before serving, toss the heads in melted butter until browning slightly and season with a little sugar or orange juice. I often part-cook endive by boiling, then braise it in the oven in cream, a sauce or stock. My favorite recipe is for Endive & Smoked Bacon Gratin (page 202) which is baked in cream flavored with Dijon mustard and cheese. Radicchio is prepared in the same way as endive, but it

turns a murky rust-brown when cooked. One of the best methods of cooking it is to cut it in half lengthwise, brush it with oil, and sear the cut leaves on a hot ridged cast iron grill pan. Serve warm with a squeeze of lemon juice and plenty of salt and freshly ground pepper.

An excellent source of vitamins C, A and B, particularly when eaten very fresh and raw. Spinach is a good source of calcium, potassium and iron, although this is "bound up" by oxalic acid and not easily available to our bodies.

Originating in ancient Persia, spinach appeared in China and then North Africa, and it was from there that it was brought by the Moors into medieval Spain. It was popular in monastic gardens throughout Europe, eventually finding its way across the English Channel. By the 16th century, its virtues of being quick, easy to grow and cook, were well known to the English.

Spinach is an annual plant which can be grown all year round, which means that if you are a gardener and plant it successionally you should never be without it. There are basically two varieties of true or real spinach, one with long-lobed leaves and the other a less hardy variety with round leaves. It is available as loose leaves with the stalks attached, or trimmed, washed and pre-packed ready for use. When selecting, make sure it is absolutely fresh as it deteriorates very quickly. The leaves should have a crisp

spinach
Spinacea oleracea

texture and be bright green in color. Check the bags in particular, paying attention to the "sell by" and "use by" dates. Store in the refrigerator and use as soon as possible.

Spinach is best when the leaves are small, young and vibrant in color, then they need very little preparation and are perfect for eating raw in a salad. Pick the spinach over and remove any damaged or discolored leaves, trimming off any thick, coarse or long stalks. Fill the sink with cold water, add some salt, then the prepared leaves. Swirl the leaves in the water to wash away any sand, dirt or grit that might be clinging to them, then if they are very gritty, drain off the water and repeat the process. If serving raw, spin-dry in a salad spinner. For cooking, lift out a large handful at a time, shake off the excess water, and pack into a very large saucepan with a lump of butter and only the water that is clinging to the leaves. Press the spinach well into the pan to get in as much as possible, cover closely blunt tips. It tastes slightly milder than true spinach. Indeed, it was these greens that Captain Cook gave his sailors to prevent scurvy, and they were introduced to the Royal Botanic Gardens at Kew in 1771 by the botanist Joseph Banks after his voyage on board the *Endeavour*.

with nonstick baking paper and clamp on the lid. Cook over a moderate heat, shaking the pan occasionally to prevent the leaves from sticking, until the spinach has collapsed and is tender. This will take 5–8 minutes. Don't overcook or the leaves will become slimy. Now your full pan of spinach will be almost empty — it is surprising just how much a large volume of leaves reduces in cooking. Remove the lid and paper, and drain the spinach in a colander or conical sieve, pressing the leaves against the sides to squeeze out the liquid (this makes a refreshing and nutritious drink.) The spinach is now ready to use. When used as an accompaniment, simply return it to the pan with a generous teaspoon of butter and season with salt and pepper and a pinch of freshly grated nutmeg. Shake over a high heat to warm through, then serve immediately.

The slightly astringent and very distinctive flavor of spinach goes well with cheese, butter, cream, and eggs. It combines well with meat and fish. It is particularly good in the fruity stews popular in Middle Eastern cooking, as well as in the pastry tarts and pies of France, Italy, and Greece. It tastes great in soups, soufflés, and purées, superb with lentils, chickpeas, beans, and potatoes, and is also popular stir-fried on its own or with other ingredients.

Not the real thing

There are two leafy greens that are not true spinach at all, but they bear the name spinach and are prepared and cooked in the same way.

New Zealand spinach (Tetragonia tetragonoides) is a useful substitute for true spinach because it can stand the hottest weather without running to seed. It has smaller and softer leaves, which are roughly triangular in shape with

Leaf beet (Beta vulgaris cicula), also called perpetual spinach or spinach beet, is easier to grow than true spinach because it is not so sensitive to drought. It is also biennial and will not run to seed. The leaves are small and oval (below) with a coarser, less delicate flavor than true spinach. They are ideal for salads.

stalks &
stems

Celery is high in potassium and raises alkaline levels in the blood, so it is good for gout and rheumatism. Low in calories, it helps reduce blood pressure and is also a diuretic.

Celery has been cultivated for many centuries. The inspiration for those first gardeners (probably Greek) was the wild celery that still flourishes close to seashores in many parts of Europe and the British Isles. Smallage, a cultivated wild celery, has been grown in continental Europe since medieval times for its flavor and medicinal properties, and the tradition of adding it to soups, broths, and stews is still very important in country areas.

There are three types of celery: smallage, with its thin green stems and head of bushy green leaves, has a strong flavor and is used mainly for its heads, which are cut off rather than dug up. Then there is the green or yellow-green self-blanching variety, most often sold in plastic sleeves. The flavor of this mass-produced product is bland and may be the reason why celery's popularity has waned. The third variety is white celery, also known as trench celery because it was originally grown in deep trenches. Its stems are blanched by being progressively covered in earth or soot, which accounts for its other name of dirty celery. It has a crisp texture and nutty flavor, and reaches a peak of availability around Christmas.

All celery should be crisp, firm and pure in color. The leaves should be fresh and lively. If the celery is to be used whole, wash under cold running water, separating the stalks slightly. Remove any strings from the stalks, trim a slice off the root end, and pull away the tough outer leaves to expose the more delicate inner heart. Trim across the stalks, leaving a bulbous head about 6 inches long. Reserve the leaves and cut off stalks for salads, broths, soups, and stews. The whole head can be boiled or braised in broth, then served with a rich white sauce or the well-reduced braising liquor. Chopped, raw celery gives a spark of life and crunch to mixed salad leaves, and has a similar effect when combined with crunchy fruit, such as apples.

Celery adds a very distinctive flavor and texture to soups and stews. Cut it into appropriate lengths and boil, braise or stew until tender. Sticks or pieces of celery are also excellent fried on their own to be combined with other ingredients, or stir-fried with other mixed vegetables.

celery

Apium graveolens

var. dulce

celery root

Apium graveolens

var. rapaceum

A storehouse of energy, celery root is high in carbohydrates, rich in iron with some quantities of vitamins C and B.

Celery root was introduced into Britain from Egypt in the early 18th century by Stephen Switzer, a writer and seedsman. Although strictly classed as a root vegetable, it is in fact a swollen stem that grows just above the ground. It is roughly spherical in shape with a knobby surface, which accounts for its other names, turnip-rooted celery and knob celery. The spindly stalks and leafy foliage are similar to smallage or soup celery, and can be used in the same way. Celery root has a distinctive nutty, slightly tangy taste similar to celery, but to my mind it is more powerful.

It is in season from October through May (any later and it is inclined to be fibrous), when you should look for smallish, firm bulbs, about the size of an orange rather than a grapefruit. Choose those with the smoothest skin you can find, because there will be less waste when peeling. Any leaves should be lively and a strong green color. The root should also look fresh. Celery root will keep well for up to a week in the vegetable compartment of the refrigerator. Before peeling, scrub thoroughly with a firm vegetable brush under cold running water to remove any dirt. Cut off the roots and any stems and leaves. Discard the roots, but reserve the stems and leaves to use as a flavoring for broths, soups, and stews. Both, if fresh and crisp, are also excellent chopped and added to salads. The skin should be peeled off using a firm sharp knife. If

you are unsure of the thickness of the skin or how much to take off, cut the celery root in half first so you can judge how much to remove. Once peeled, celery root turns brown quickly. To prevent this, place it immediately in cold water mixed with the juice of ½ lemon or 1–2 tablespoons of white vinegar. This is known as acidulated water. Prepare celery root in cubes, chunks, sticks, or crisps, whichever the recipe requires.

Celery root is usually cooked by boiling in acidulated water until tender. It is then drained, tossed in butter, and served as a side-dish. Celery root can also be mashed after boiling and served like mashed potato. It can be roasted in chunks, cut into French fries, sliced and deep-fried like potato chips, or shredded or grated with raw potatoes, shaped into pancakes, and fried. Cut into cubes, it is used in soups and stews. Celery root is also used raw in salads, such as the French *rémoulade du céleri-rave*, thin sticks of celery root mixed with mayonnaise.

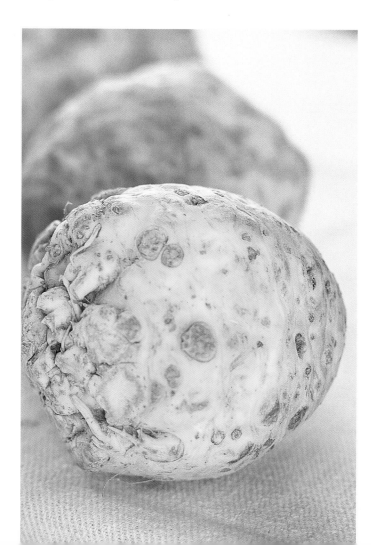

asparagus
Asparagus officinalis

Asparagus is low in calories, a rich source of vitamins A, B2 and C, and a moderate source of E. It is also high in potassium, folic acid, calcium, and iron.

The season for this delicate yet distinctively flavored vegetable lasts only 4 months, from March through June. At other times of the year, asparagus is imported from Thailand, Hungary, Holland, and Cyprus. Its short season makes it something not to tire of or take for granted, so take advantage of it while you can.

Wild asparagus has grown along the river banks and seashores of southern Europe, Asia, and northwest Africa for centuries, and thrived in the dry meadows, sand dunes, limestone cliffs and volcanic hills of northern Europe. It was favored by the Greeks and cultivated by the Romans. It was elevated to the vegetable pantheon by aristocrats at the court of Louis XV in France, in particular by his mistress, Madame de Pompadour, who believed, as many people still do, that it had aphrodisiac powers. But that is not all asparagus is noted for. It has traditionally been used in folk medicine as a tonic and sedative and has been recommended for treating rheumatism, poor eyesight and toothache; it is also a diuretic.

Asparagus is a member of the lily family. It is available in three varieties: green, white, and purple. Green-stemmed asparagus, mainly grown and certainly preferred in Britain, North America, Italy, and France, is allowed to grow naturally into the light before being harvested when it is about 6 inches tall. It is graded into three sizes: "special", very thick, juicy prime asparagus; "medium",

about ½ inch in diameter and good for most recipes; and "sprue", the short spindly type that is very tender, cooks quickly and is particularly good for broiling and stir-frying. Green asparagus is also produced in France, Thailand, Holland, and Cyprus. White asparagus, which has a creamy white stalk and ivory tips, is favored by the Spanish, and also by the Dutch, Germans, and Italians. It is grown under mounds of soil and cut just as the tips begin to show. Purple or violet asparagus is mostly grown in France. The spears are cut once the tips have grown about 1½ inches above the ground, consequently the stalks are white and the tops tinged with purple or green.

As with many delicate plants, asparagus is at its best when eaten as fresh as possible. Deterioration is rapid once it is picked. Harvesting asparagus from your own garden is the best way to enjoy it, but this is not always possible. When buying, look for firm, straight and sprightly spears, the tips tightly furled.

Unless the asparagus comes straight from the garden, cut off the bottom or "butt" end of the stalk, removing ½–1 inch of any hard, dried or woody parts. With freshly pulled asparagus this is not necessary, and sprue hardly needs trimming at all. Like this it is perfect eaten raw with rock salt and perhaps a squeeze of lemon juice, some balsamic vinegar and extra virgin olive oil.

To prepare asparagus for cooking, use a small serrated knife or vegetable peeler, start about 2 inches below the tip and peel down to the butt. This will expose the tender flesh of the stalk and enable it to cook in the same time as the delicate tip. If you are using baby asparagus, you will only need to trim the base of each stalk.

Asparagus can be prepared in advance to this point, wrapped in wax paper or foil and stored in the bottom of the refrigerator for a few hours.

To cook asparagus, bring a large, shallow skillet, sauté pan, or oval casserole full of water to a boil. Add 1 tablespoon salt and lay the asparagus in a single layer over the bottom of the pan so that it is completely covered with water. Cover with a lid and quickly return to a boil. Remove the lid and boil for 5 minutes. Test to see if the asparagus is tender by spearing the stalk with the point of a sharp knife. If it is not tender, cook for another minute and test again, continuing to do this until the asparagus is ready. Lift quickly from the water using tongs and place on paper towels to drain, then serve immediately. For an entirely different taste and texture, fine asparagus spears or sprue can be broiled on a ridged cast iron grill pan, seasoned with salt and pepper, and given a lift with a dash of lemon juice.

Simplicity of serving is always the best for asparagus. Its flavor should be coaxed out and enhanced, not overpowered. All it needs is some melted butter, rock salt and freshly ground black pepper or, for a change, a dressing of balsamic vinegar, a little extra virgin oil and maybe a shaving or two of Parmesan cheese. It is delicious with Hollandaise Sauce (page 233.) One of my favorite dishes is Asparagus & White Wine Risotto (page 143), but asparagus also tastes good in soups, quiches, pancakes, and gratins, with scrambled eggs, wrapped in Parma ham, stirred into omelets, and served cold with mayonnaise.

Kohlrabi is rich in vitamin C, with traces of minerals, particularly potassium, and fiber.

Although it is also known as turnip-rooted cabbage, kohlrabi is not a root, but the swollen part of the lower stem. It is a most interesting looking vegetable, with its green or purple bulbous stem and bizarrely shaped leaf shoots sticking out from it — rather like a visitor from another planet. It is much more distinctive than the turnip or swede which it resembles in flavor. Kohlrabi has been cultivated in continental Europe since the 17th century, and is particularly popular in Germany and Switzerland. It is also widely available in India, China, and other parts of Asia. There are two varieties, the pale green and the purple. In flavor they are akin to turnip and cabbage but more refined, with the additional hint of exotic flavors — water-chestnut and celery root. A word of warning: these subtleties can be lost if kohlrabi is overcooked.

The swollen kohlrabi stem can grow to the size of a grapefruit, but it is best eaten when much smaller, no bigger than a small orange or a large beefsteak tomato — when too large it tends to be coarse, woody, and fibrous. Its skin should look fresh, with a rich bloom. Kohlrabi will keep well for just over a week if stored in the bottom of the refrigerator or in a cool place.

To prepare kohlrabi for cooking, trim away the leaves and reserve them if you like, to be boiled like spinach or stir-fried like leafy greens. Peel off a thin layer of skin, then cut the kohlrabi into cubes, sticks, or slices as the recipe

kohlrabi

Brassica oleracea

Gongylodes group

requires. It can be sliced into thicker sticks or chips and deep-fried, or cut into very thin slices and fried like potato chips. It can be cut into wedges, blanched until almost tender, drained, and refreshed, then served as part of a raw vegetable platter. Diced or cubed, kohlrabi can be added to soups and stews, boiled like turnips, and served with butter and salt and pepper, or mashed like potatoes. It is also good topped with cheese and bread crumbs and made into a gratin, or roasted with other root vegetables. The crispness and pure flavor of raw kohlrabi can be enjoyed like celery root, cut into very thin sticks or grated, added to a salad or mixed with vinaigrette.

Botanically and nutritionally similar to the globe artichoke, the cardoon is also rich in potassium.

The cardoon is a giant edible thistle closely related to the globe artichoke, found wild in much of North Africa and the Mediterranean. It has bold, spiky silver green foliage and tall thistle-like purple flower heads, smaller and more compact than the globe artichoke, but equally stunning. Cultivated plants often grow to 6 feet in height and are valued not only as a vegetable but as an attractive garden plant. Unlike the globe artichoke, the cardoon is grown for its succulent leaf stalks rather than its flower head. The leaves look rather like very long celery and are blanched when they reach maturity, in order to retain their pale green color.

The history of the cardoon is sketchy, but it is thought to have been held in high esteem by the Romans before the birth of Christ. Nowadays it is extremely popular in Spain, southern France, Italy, and Morocco. Cardoons are cooked in much the same way as celery but only the inner ribs and hearts are used, the outer stalks and leaves being too tough and stringy. Their flavor is somewhere between celery, globe artichoke and asparagus.

To prepare, cut away the leaves, roots, and prickly outer stems, leaving the inner stalks and firm succulent heart. Wash well under cold running water and remove any strings. Trim and cut into manageable lengths, then put them immediately into cold acidulated water to prevent discoloration. Very young stems may be tender enough to eat in a raw vegetable platter, in which case, cut them into 6-inch lengths. One of the most famous sauces served with cardoons is *bagna cauda*, a rich warm combination of anchovies, olive oil and butter from Piedmont in Italy. If you feel the stalks are not quite tender enough to eat raw, drop them into boiling salted and acidulated water for 4–5 minutes to tenderize them slightly. This will also remove any trace of bitterness. Drain, refresh under running water until cold, then dry before serving. To fully cook the stems, boil them for up to 30 minutes until they are tender. Drain well and serve with melted butter, olive oil or vinaigrette, and salt and pepper. They also taste good with anchovies and shavings of Parmesan, or simply with butter, cream, and cheese, and can be used in most recipes for braised celery or fennel.

cardoon
Cynara cardunculus

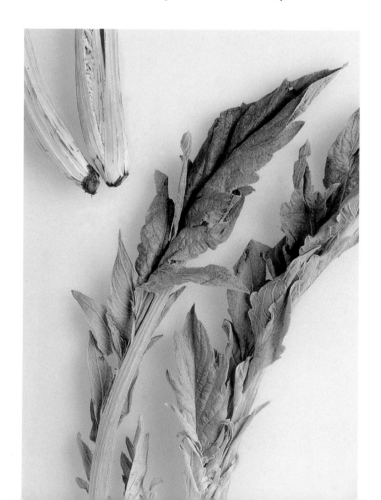

globe artichoke

Cynara scolymus

Composed almost entirely of water but with a little carbohydrate, iodine, and iron, globe artichokes are a dieter's dream.

One of the great joys of my vegetable garden in County Down is the corner where globe artichokes grow beside the gooseberry bush. They make a spectacular show. The huge bluey-purple thistle heads and big jagged green leaves look so striking against the white of a lime-washed wall and the spectacular backdrop of the muted blues and purples of the Mourne Mountains. I enjoy their visual beauty as much as their taste, and make sure that I grow enough to satisfy both plate and vase.

The globe artichoke is an edible thistle, a close relative of the cotton thistle and the cardoon. Given its Arab name, *al-kharshuf*, it is thought to have originated in North Africa, whence it found its way to southern Europe where it still grows wild. It has been prized by many for centuries, particularly by the Greeks and Romans, but it is believed to have been the Italians who were responsible for its popularity in the courts of Renaissance Europe. The globe artichoke reached England in the 16th century, and rapidly became a popular feature in kitchen gardens.

The artichoke flourishes in a light sandy soil and a mild climate. The flower buds are edible at various stages of the plant's maturity — but if you eat them, there will be no flowers. The plant grows to about 4–5 feet tall with a 3-foot spread of attractive leaves, which range in color from brilliant bottle green to silvery gray-green and are topped with large thistle-like flowers. There are two main types, green and purple. Either color can be round or egg-shaped and there is no marked difference in the flavor.

If you grow your own artichokes, harvest them when they are young and the flower buds small, then they can be eaten raw or lightly broiled while they are delicate and tender. If you prefer artichokes boiled or steamed, allow them to grow slightly larger. However you prefer to eat artichokes, harvest them only just before use. Whether picked straight from the garden or selected from the supermarket shelf, globe artichokes should be bright in color, whether green or purple. The leaves on the flower heads should be firm and fleshy, forming a tightly shaped globe. They should have a healthy bloom, feel heavy and be of an even size.

To prepare artichokes, soak them, stem-side up, for about 15 minutes in a large bowl or bucket of cold water to which the juice of a lemon or a few tablespoons of white wine vinegar have been added, then wash in cold running water. Drain and continue the preparation.

Small artichokes If very small, remove the leaves from the base, trim the stem to about 1 inch and peel it. The stem is very tender and can be eaten. The hairy choke has not yet formed, so the inner yellow leaves can be gouged out with a knife. Keep the artichokes in acidulated water, then drain, slice and eat raw with vinaigrette or anchoïade (anchovy sauce), or sprinkle the slices with lemon juice and add to a leafy salad. Artichokes can also be braised until tender, or quartered and fried in olive oil with a little garlic, then served with a dash of lemon juice and a sprinkling of rock salt.

To eat artichokes Pull away the artichoke leaves one at a time, starting at the bottom. Dip the tender base into some butter or sauce, then draw the leaf through your teeth, squeezing out and eating the fleshy part. Discard the rest. When most of the leaves have been eaten, you will come to a few thin pale-colored pointed leaves which can be pulled off in one piece. Nibble around these. This will leave a hairy mound like a haystack, topping a fleshy saucer-shaped heart – this is the most delicious part called the choke. Slide your knife between the hairs and the bottom and, holding both the knife and choke between finger and thumb, pull out the "hay" in sections. Discard the hay and eat the heart.

The fleshy heart is often eaten by itself as a delicacy. It can be taken from the cooked artichoke once the leaves have been discarded, but can easily become overcooked and discolored. To prevent this, I prepare them raw, which is the Italian and French way. Have ready a large bowl of acidulated water. Wash and drain the artichokes and break off the stems. Holding the artichoke by the head, bottom up, bend a lower leaf back on itself until it snaps, then peel it off towards the base, leaving the meaty part attached. Do this until you are left with a cone of fine central leaves which can be pulled out in one piece and removed with the choke. As you remove the leaves, rub the cut surfaces with lemon juice, then drop the hearts into acidulated water. Drop the hearts into boiling salted water to which the juice of a lemon and some olive oil have been added. Return to a boil and cook for 15–20 minutes until they can be pierced easily with the point of a knife.

Artichoke hearts taste good with hollandaise sauce, butter or vinaigrette, with a garlic or anchovy-flavored sauce, or simply with thick plain yogurt sharpened with lemon juice. They can also be fried in butter, or sliced and added to salads, gratins, and even scrambled eggs.

Medium artichokes If the stems are long, break them off close to the base – this will pull away the tough fibers from the heart. Remove any small or withered leaves from the base and rub the exposed surfaces with lemon juice. Put the artichokes into a very large pan of boiling salted water to which about 2 tablespoons of white wine vinegar or lemon juice have been added for every 2½ pints of water. Set a wire cake rack or a double layer of cheesecloth on top of them to hold them down and boil, uncovered, over a high heat for 30–45 minutes. They are ready when the leaves at the base can be easily removed and feel tender. Use tongs to transfer them to a colander, arranging the heads pointing down so the water drains out. Serve hot with melted butter, Hollandaise Sauce (page 233) or vinaigrette, or cold with vinaigrette or mayonnaise.

The fennel bulb has a high water content. It is low in calories and rich in the vitamins A and E. It is also a good source of calcium and potassium and aids digestion.

Sweet fennel, Italian fennel, and Florence fennel are all romantic aliases for this decorative garden vegetable. The herb, common fennel, has a lineage stretching back to ancient times around the Aegean and the Mediterranean, where it grew wild and was used both for flavoring and medicinal purposes. In contrast, the vegetable's popularity is quite recent, stretching back no more than 300 years in Italy and to the 18th century in Britain.

Fennel, the vegetable, is grown primarily for its aniseed-flavored bulb, which develops from the swollen base of the stalks. These broad, curved, fleshy leaf stalks overlap to form a firm pale green or white crisp head about 3–4 inches across. Growing out of these is a mass of bright green feathery foliage. The bulbs sit on top of the soil, their tiny roots filtering down into the earth and their feathery heads stretching sometimes to 2 feet tall. There are male and female bulbs. The short, squat ones are female, the more elegant, elongated variety the male. Baby fennel (opposite) are particularly attractive.

When buying fennel, choose firm bulbs which are pale in color, have tightly packed leaf stalks and fluffy green foliage. Smaller bulbs are less wasteful as the outer leaves are less fibrous and not so much trimming is required.

Fennel is the perfect salad vegetable. It is crisp like celery, but with a clearer, more distinctive flavor. It does not discolor when it is cut and, if slightly limp, can be

fennel
Foeniculum vulgare

revived by steeping in a bowl of iced water for about an hour. To use the bulb whole or in halves, do not cut off the base because it holds the fleshy stalks together. Just tidy it up by shaving off a few slivers with a vegetable peeler. Rinse under cold running water, dry, then use as the recipe requires. To give a crisp texture through a leafy salad, cut the fennel across into thin rings. When it is to be used like celery and eaten with fruit and cheese or served as part of a raw vegetable platter, cut it downward into strips. Alternatively, it can be cut into wedges or just torn off into individual stalks, the base end trimmed, and served with fruit, Parmesan or pecorino cheese — a popular way of serving it in Italy. To include in a crisp salad, cut or chop it into smallish pieces. Any trimmings from the base or fibrous stalks can be removed and reserved for fish or chicken stock or soup. The stalks can also be cut off, chopped and used for broth, soup or stuffings, or dried and used to perfume the smoke of a barbecue fire — this is good when grilling fish and vegetables.

Fennel can be boiled whole, served with melted butter and garnished with chopped fennel heads. Puréed, it can be used for a soufflé or sauce. Blanched fennel can be tossed in butter until it begins to brown slightly, then finished with a little Pernod and cream and a sprinkling of chopped fennel. My own favorite is quite simple: par-boil, then sprinkle with Parmesan, and brown under the broiler. Raw or blanched fennel can be added to stir-fries or sautéed and added to stews. It is delicious as part of a selection of sautéed diced vegetables and is good with tomato-based sauces, garlic, and olives. Cut into quarters, it is excellent broiled. Place the pieces, flat-side down, on a hot ridged cast iron grill pan and cook for about 5 minutes on each side. Don't fiddle with it or the sections will fall apart, and turn it carefully when ready.

the onion
family

A source of vitamins A, B, C, and E, calcium, phosphorus, potassium, iron, sodium, sulfur, and copper in small amounts.

Onions are thought to have originated in the Middle East. Fresh and dried onions were eaten in Old Testament times, and the Bible records that they were one of the foods the Israelites longed for in the wilderness. They were common in ancient Egypt, and were thought to be invested with supernatural powers. Onion bulbs and wooden models of onions have been found in tombs in the Valley of the Kings at Luxor and we are told that the main diet of the workers who built the pyramids at Giza consisted of radishes, garlic, and onions.

Throughout the Middle Ages, onions were unrivaled for both flavor and substance, in soups, broths, and stews, but it was for their supposed medicinal value that they were most highly prized, and they were used to alleviate many ailments. By the 18th century, they were grown in almost every country garden in England. These days we know that onions pack a real vitamin and mineral punch, that they contain an antiseptic oil and an anticoagulant, and can help to lower cholesterol levels in the blood. There are over 300 different varieties.

onion

Allium cepa

Pickling onions Also known as baby onions and button onions, pickling onions are a small variety of yellow onion, bulbous, elongated, and slightly flattened in shape. In some varieties the flesh is clearly tinged with yellow. They are used for home pickling, adding whole to stews, sautéing in butter, and roasting. They can also be caramelized, used whole in pies, and threaded onto skewers for broiling.

Red onions (opposite page) Sometimes called Mexican or salad onions, these have a mild sweet flavor and can be eaten raw, thinly sliced or chopped in salads or salsas. They are very attractive, with ruby-red papery skin and pink-tinged flesh. They are of medium size and slightly squat, elongated, or torpedo-shaped.

Spanish or **Bermuda onions** (page 44) A large variety of yellow onion with a rich copper-colored skin. Mild and sweet, they are excellent for general cooking and for using raw in salads. Their size makes them useful for baking.

Green onions (scallions) (page 48) These are onions grown from seed and harvested very young, before their green shoots have had time to mature and wither. They are white skinned with small, slightly flattened bulbs at the base of slim green stalks. They can have either a mild delicate flavor or a more pungent peppery taste and are generally eaten raw. Chopped (both the white and green parts), they are added to salads, salsas, and dressings, cooked and stirred into mashed potatoes, added to egg dishes for color and flavor, and included in stir-fries.

Vidalia onions These are named for Vidalia, Georgia, where they thrive. They are large, pale, and juicy, with a mild, sweet flavor. They are good roasted, excellent with a light creamy sauce, and are also eaten raw in salads.

Yellow onions The name is misleading because the skin is more golden-brown than yellow. A good all-purpose onion, which comes in two sizes: large and medium–small. It is the variety that you will find everywhere throughout the year. These are thought to be the most pungent of the onions, but I find they vary slightly, depending on type.

White onions These are available all year around in all shapes and sizes. The flavor varies from very strong to mild. The very small, mild onions with silver skins are called Paris Silver Skin and can be added whole to stews, or served in a creamy white sauce.

Onions are available all year around and, although they will change with the seasons, their characteristic flavor is always present. If you grow your own, they can be stored throughout the winter, or you can buy a string of onions and hang them up in a dark dry place for months, but they are so readily available that it is not really necessary to store them. When you buy them, make sure they are firm, with papery, dry, crackly skins. They should not have begun to sprout.

   Once an onion is cut, it deteriorates rapidly as well as tainting everything near it, so don't store cut onions, even for a short time. Select the size you need so there will be no

To slice an onion Peel the onion leaving the root attached, then slice either in whole rings the thickness that the recipe requires, or cut the onion in half lengthwise through the root, then slice it into half rings, working toward the root.

To mince an onion Set the peeled onion on a board. With a sharp knife, cut the onion in half lengthwise through the root, leaving the root attached. Set one half cut-side down on the board with the root facing the hand that is not holding the knife. Starting nearest to the board and working upward to the rounded side, make a series of horizontal cuts from the shoot end of the onion toward the root but not through it. The closer you keep these cuts together the more finely minced the onion will be. Turn the onion so the root is away from you. Working from the center to the sides, make cuts down through the onion onto the board. Turn the onion back to its original position and slice across the onion from the shoot to the root, again keeping the cuts close together to obtain fine dice. The flesh will fall apart into small pieces and come away from the root, which can either be discarded or added to the stockpot. If necessary, chop through the onion to make finer dice. Repeat with the other onion half.

Onion juice Cut a peeled onion in half and scrape the cut surface with a broad-bladed kitchen knife over a bowl to release the onion juice. Alternatively, grate the onion on the largest section of a grater and, with the back of a spoon, squeeze the juice out of the grated flesh.

waste. The general preparation is the same regardless of the variety of onion. First remove the skin, unless you are intending to either roast the onion whole in its skin or add it to a broth, to which it will impart a rich golden color. Remove the skin by pulling it away from the stalk end, then peeling it off in layers to expose the flesh. Trim the roots but do not cut them off at this stage; they will help hold the onion together while you either slice or chop it. Baby, pickling, or silver skin onions have very tight skin, which can be difficult to remove in the normal way. For speed and convenience, drop these into a pan of boiling water and cook for 1 minute, then drain and refresh under cold water. Gently remove the skin. Trim off the root close to the flesh, but don't detach it completely or the onion will fall apart.

Onions can be cooked in a variety of ways. They can be fried in butter or oil, cut into rings, slices, or dice, to be added to soups, stews, risottos, omelets, and pilafs, sweated until meltingly tender and used as the filling for tarts, or puréed and made into a sauce. The frying can be slow, over a low heat to soften and tenderize without coloring them, or fast and furious, to caramelize and brown them. Sautéed onions are an ideal accompaniment or garnish for fried or broiled meats. They can be sliced into rings, dipped in milk and flour or batter, and then deep-fried. Small whole onions can be boiled and served in a white sauce or tossed in butter and sugar until caramelized. Small and medium onions can be roasted whole, with or without their skin, while larger onions can be stuffed and baked to make a substantial meal.

shallot
Allium cepa
Aggregatum group

Shallots are a good source of vitamins A, B, C, and E. They contain small quantities of calcium, phosphorus, potassium, iron, sodium, sulfur, and copper.

I have a cluster of shallots, a string of garlic, and a bunch of bay leaves hanging on the dresser in my kitchen. To my mind, the shallot is an icon of continental cooking. The French, in particular, are noted for their use of shallots when making the sauces for which Cordon Bleu cuisine has become famous.

The shallot is not a baby onion. It is a member of the onion family, with very distinct characteristics. It grows in small, tight clusters like garlic, with anything from 2–6 bulbs grouped together and joined at the root. The single bulbs vary in shape, but are generally smaller, slimmer, flatter and, in some cases, pear-shaped and more elongated than the common onion. The flavor is neither onion nor garlic, but it has similarities to both. It is definite and strong but without an excessively fiery taste, and its subtle mildness and lack of heavy smell makes it perfect for eating raw.

There are three main varieties of shallot. The most common is the bronzed, golden-yellow shallot (right), which is slightly larger than the others and keeps well. Then there is the *échalote rosé* (left), a small and pretty pinkish-red shallot, which to my taste has the best flavor. The third kind is the smallish, gray-brown shallot, known by the French as *échalote gris*. This has a pronounced, concentrated flavor and is mostly used for sauces.

Shallots should be firm without any green shoots, their outer skin crisp, papery, and fresh. Most shallots are sold in small quantities in net bags, bunches, or strings which can be hung up for storage, although they can also be bought loose. They keep for several months in a cool, dry, well-ventilated place.

The shallot is suited to the making and flavoring of sauces because of its subtlety of flavor and the way in which its tender flesh cooks to such softness. The most famous of the shallot sauces is bordelaise. Minced shallots and Bordeaux wine are cooked together to concentrate their flavors before being used as a base for this rich and distinctive sauce, traditionally served with broiled entrecôte steak.

Like garlic and onions, whole shallots can be roasted with or without their skins until they are meltingly tender, or cooked around a roast. They can also be boiled in milk, or cooked gently in butter or oil. Mashed to a purée, the cooked shallot flesh can be used as the basis of a sauce or stirred into butter as a flavoring and garnish for broiled meats. Whole raw peeled shallots can be added to stews and casseroles to give extra flavor and texture, or they can be pickled. Minced raw shallots can be blended with butter as a flavoring, eaten raw in salads, or used instead of onions when only a small amount is required. Young shallot leaves can be minced and used as a garnish for salads.

leek

Allium porrum

Contains small amounts of iron, potassium, vitamin C, and protein.

The leek has a very long history, stretching back well over 5,000 years to the ancient Egyptians, the Greeks, and the Romans. It has been grown in Britain for the best part of 2,000 years and valued as a vegetable to provide bulk for the poor man's pot — it has been called the poor man's asparagus. In medieval times, the leek was favored for its medicinal value as a diuretic. Its association with the Welsh can be traced back over 1,400 years, when it was adopted as an emblem to commemorate a famous victory over the Anglo-Saxons.

Leeks can withstand wintry rain, frost, and snow, and are the principal vegetable in the winter garden, standing alone when everything else has been harvested. Like the onion, the leek has a tight root structure at its base. It is long and elegant, measuring between 8–12 inches tall, and about ¾–2 inches across. In flavor it is milder than the onion and makes an excellent aromatic or onion substitute in many recipes for stews and casseroles.

When choosing leeks, opt for the smallest you can find and chose those of similar size, particularly if they are to be used whole. When picked small, leeks are tender and mildly aromatic. Make sure that the white part is really white, and that it feels firm. The leaves should be tightly rolled around each other and have a rich green color.

If leeks have dirt clinging to them, prepare them before storing. Cut off and discard any muddy roots, then trim away wilted or green tops, saving these in a plastic bag for the soup-pot. Put the whole leeks in a loose-fitting plastic bag and store in the bottom of the refrigerator. Only wash leeks at this stage if they are very dirty, then dry them well. If storing prepackaged leeks, transfer them to a plastic bag in which they can breathe. Leeks deteriorate rapidly, so keep for only 3–5 days. They can taint other foods, so keep them away from butter, milk, and cream.

Before cooking, all leeks need careful preparation because they tend to trap dirt and grit in their folds. Remove and discard the roots if this has not been done already, then remove the coarse, deep green ends of the leaves and the outer layer of white flesh along with its darker green tops. All of this is full of flavor and can be chopped and used for broth. If you are going to slice the leek across into rings, do so now, then wash them well in a colander under cold running water. If you need the white part only, with perhaps a little of the pale green leaves attached, cut off accordingly. If the leek is to be left whole, make a cut from the trimmed end halfway down its length, then hold leaf-end down under cold running water, gently opening out the leaves and allowing the dirt and grit to wash away. Shake well. Wash the leek, or chop it first, then wash. If you are not intending to use all of the leek at once, only wash the amount you require and store the rest, unwashed, in a plastic bag in the vegetable compartment of the refrigerator.

Trimmed whole leeks can be steamed or boiled in the minimum amount of water for 5–20 minutes, depending on thickness. They should be just tender, with a slight resistance when skewered with the point of a knife. Keep testing them as overcooked leeks are unappetizing and slimy. Leeks can be served simply with butter and seasoned with salt and pepper, coated with cream and herbs, or dressed while warm in a light vinaigrette and served cold as a salad. They can be lightly boiled, then coated in cheese sauce and cooked *au gratin* in the oven or under the broiler, or layered with cheese and covered with cream, then baked in the oven and finished under the broiler. Leeks can also be braised gently in butter or oil and perhaps a little wine or broth, with thyme or bay leaf to season. This can be done in a heavy casserole or shallow skillet with a tight-fitting lid; cook the leeks slowly until tender. The juices can be made into a light sauce with the addition of some butter, *beurre manié*, or thick cream. Leeks are also compatible with lemon juice, paprika, caraway, and coriander (cilantro) seeds.

Sliced across into pieces 2–3 inches wide, leeks can be gently fried in butter or oil until softened, then used in a gratin or gently stir-fried with garlic, chili pepper, and grated fresh ginger, then moistened with a little water, dry sherry, and soy sauce. They can be sliced across in rings (both the white and green parts), fried until soft in butter and oil without coloring, and used as a base for a tart or quiche, sauce, or soup. A traditional way of using leeks is in stews and soups such as vichyssoise or cock-a-leekie. They also make an impressive garnish for roast or broiled fish or meat. Cut the leek into thread-like strips about 3 inches long, then deep-fry them until pale golden. The strands will curl and look like delicate pieces of straw.

garlic
Allium sativum

Contains small quantities of vitamin C and minerals, calcium, phosphorus, potassium, and iron.

I well remember my larger-than-life art teacher at school inviting groups of us to her home. These were inspiring occasions, although the odor, a mix of perfume, face powder, and garlic, was almost overpowering. She was certainly ahead of her time. Today, garlic's image is of a crucial flavoring for so many dishes now familiar to us from around the world, and as a medicinal warrior doing battle with harmful bacteria, bolstering the body's immune system and lowering cholesterol levels.

Garlic seems to have originated in Asia Minor, and it was held in awe by the Egyptians, Greeks, and Romans as both food, medicine and talisman to guard against evil and misfortune — thousands of years before Count Dracula and his vampire cohorts slid across our movie screens. Garlic bulbs have been found in ancient Egyptian tombs, and we know that the workers who toiled to build the pyramids demanded garlic in their diet. The use of garlic spread throughout continental Asia and the Mediterranean basin, and its popularity today is largely due to our relatively recent liking for Mediterranean, Indian and Asian cooking.

There are many different varieties, but they are all composed of a compact bulb, often described as a head, which grows below the soil and gives rise to fine green shoots. These can grow to a height of 3 feet, finishing with a flourish in a mass of white blooms. The bulbs are white, pink or purple tinged, and comprise a number of almond-shaped segments called cloves. Each of these cloves is encased in a delicate paper-like skin, held tightly together by both a communal root structure and layers of skin. As a general guide, the bigger the garlic bulb the milder the flavor.

In most places, garlic bulbs are bought cured or semi-cured, that is dried. The bulbs are harvested when the tops are beginning to dry out, then hung up until the skin becomes papery. The individual cloves are still juicy and will keep in this condition for many months in a cool, dry place. Fresh garlic, also referred to as green or wet garlic, is available around June and July. This is newly pulled garlic, with large heads of cloves. It will still have its growing stem attached, will look a little green and have moist, pliable skin. Delightfully juicy and more delicate in flavor than dried garlic, it is good sliced in salads. Don't buy too much at a time as it does not keep very well. Dried garlic is available throughout the year and can keep for several months if stored in a cool, dry place. Garlic does not keep well in the refrigerator, because the damp air causes it to sprout, but if kept in too warm conditions, the cloves will shrivel up and turn to gray powder. Whatever the variety of garlic, choose firm, plump bulbs that feel heavy for their size. The skin should be clean, dry, crisp, and unbroken. The bulbs should not have started to sprout.

To prepare garlic, remove the number of cloves you require from the bulb — these can vary in size and pungency depending on the type of garlic, so if they taste mild, you may want to add more than the recipe suggests. Peel away the papery skin surrounding each clove, then prepare according to recipe requirements. The more finely the garlic is sliced, chopped or crushed, the more juice is released and the stronger the flavor. When sliced it will be milder, when left whole, much less pungent. In fact, cooked whole garlic has a gentle, nutty flavor.

Raw chopped or sliced garlic can be added to salads and dressings and provides a mild, fresh taste. Whole, sliced, chopped or crushed, it can be stirred into stews or casseroles, soups and broths. To attenuate the flavor, it can be sautéed first, but take care not to let it burn or it will be unpleasantly bitter. If frying with onions which need to be browned, add the garlic once the onions are brown, and fry only for a few minutes to soften without coloring.

Crushed raw garlic can be mixed with softened butter, minced parsley, and lemon juice, and seasoned with salt and pepper to create a wonderful garlic butter. This can then be served with vegetables or pasta, spread on bread to be baked, broiled, or roasted, or used as the French do to

"drown" snails. I use 6–12 garlic cloves to 4–8 tablespoons butter. A small lump of garlic butter tastes good melting over broiled salmon steaks.

Whole cloves of garlic or complete bulbs in their skins can be roasted in a preheated 375 degree oven for about 30 minutes until tender, either on their own, in a little oil or around a roast. Roasted garlic is sweet and succulent, with a mellow flavor. After roasting, the skins can easily be removed and the soft garlic segments released. Peeled cloves of garlic can be poached in milk or water to remove some of their fiery flavor, or if the tender cloves are required for a sauce or purée. It will take about 10 minutes to soften the cloves, which can then be crushed or processed to form a spreadable purée. The cooking liquor can be used to dilute the purée, added to soup, or enriched with egg yolk to make a sauce.

roots & tubers

cooked if they feel tender when pierced with a skewer, and when the skin is easily removed by pushing with the fingers. Cool slightly, then peel the skin and top and tail.

Serve small boiled beets whole and hot, with lots of butter and a sprinkling of herbs like chives, parsley or dill, with aïoli, anchovy dip, sweet and sour sauce, natural yogurt or sour cream. Or slice or dice them and toss in a light garlic vinaigrette, or top with a creamy white sauce flavored with horseradish. When cold, they marry well with orange segments, chopped apples, dates, dried apricots, raisins, walnuts, and pine nuts. Peeled cooked beets can be puréed, seasoned with salt, pepper, and herb vinegar and served hot, on their own or mixed with an equal quantity of mashed potato. Above all, beets make wonderful soup, such as the classic Russian borsht.

The roots of red beets are a good source of vitamins A and C, folic acid, and potassium and they are high in sugar. The leaves are rich in iron, calcium, and vitamins A and C.

This all-year-around vegetable was enjoyed in ancient times — the Greeks ate the leaves and the root was included in the Roman diet. Nowadays, beets are grown primarily for their bulbous roots, but the leaves should not be ignored and can be prepared and eaten like spinach. The root can be round, globe-shaped, oval or tapered. In color it can vary from ruby-red through golden yellow to white.

Pick or buy raw beets when small, about the size of a golf ball, then they will be tender and sweet. If the leaves are missing, make sure there is about 2 inches of stalk left on or the beets will lose color and flavor during cooking. The skin should be smooth, firm and intact. Cut off the leaves to within 2 inches of the root, wash the earth off the root, gently scrubbing if necessary. Do not trim off the actual roots. Beets are also available boiled, often peeled and in vacuum packs, sometimes preserved in vinegar.

To cook whole raw beets, simmer in a pan of water with a good squeeze of lemon juice until tender, 1–2 hours depending on size. Or bake in a tightly covered roasting dish with 4–5 tablespoons water at 350 degrees for 2–3 hours. Individual beets can be tightly wrapped in aluminum foil and baked in the same way. The beets are

beet

Beta vulgaris

Rich in vitamin C, calcium, and niacin.

Turnip is a root vegetable belonging to the cabbage family, said to have been introduced into England by the Romans. Although grown mainly for its root, the leaves of young turnips are tender, and have a peppery taste. In the South and in continental Europe these are called turnip greens, and are cooked like other leafy greens.

The root itself varies in size, shape and color. It may be white, creamy white, or streaked pinkish purple, yellowy green or green and white. Its shape is usually round or conical, 2–3 inches across, but some varieties, like the carrot-shaped French *vertus*, are longer. The young spring and summer turnips are often no larger than ping-pong balls and are sold tied up in bunches or laid out in boxes (above right), with their leaves still attached. French *navets* are small, round turnips tinged with pink or purple that have a sweet delicate flavor. The flesh of all turnips is generally white, but some may have a yellow tinge. The flavor is sweet and nutty when young and small; with age, it deepens in strength and loses some sweetness.

Choose turnips no larger than a tennis ball, with smooth, firm skin (page 56). These do not need to be peeled, just wash and scrub them. Cut any leaves off ½ inch away from the root, leaving some stalk intact. Store the leaves in a plastic bag in the refrigerator to use later as leafy greens. Larger turnips need to be peeled.

Boil turnips in just enough water to cover until just tender, this should take 10–15 minutes. Small turnips can be cooked whole, then tossed in butter, seasoned with salt and pepper and served just as they are or with ground cinnamon, ginger or mace. They can also be broiled and served with dipping sauces. When cooking large turnips, dice or slice them, then boil and finish in the same way as

turnip
Brassica campestrio
Rapifera group

small turnips, or combine them with carrots or parsnips. If dried well after draining, they can be mashed and seasoned with salt, pepper and nutmeg, on their own or with parsnips. Peeled, quartered and cubed, turnips can be added to soups and stews. They can be left whole, then peeled and cut into pieces and roasted. Blanch sliced turnips for 3–5 minutes, then fry in butter or oil flavored with garlic. Blanched turnips make an excellent salad when tossed in a light or garlic vinaigrette.

rutabaga

Brassica napus

Napobrassica group

white. All rutabagas have pale orange flesh (in contrast to the white flesh of turnips) and their flavor is sweet and nutty, with slightly stronger cabbage undertones than the turnip.

Look for small specimens that are firm and smooth, solid and heavy for their size. Remove the skin with a firm serrated-edged knife rather than a potato peeler, then cut the flesh into slices, chunks, dice or fingers using a large, firm-bladed cook's knife. Take care if the rutabaga is old because it can be very tough and resistant.

Rutabagas are ninety per cent water, and so need careful cooking. Steam or boil them in just enough water to cover until very tender. They are not pleasant to eat when even slightly undercooked, but take care because they can quickly go from undercooked to overcooked. Drain well, return to the pan, and cover with foil. Allow to dry before tossing in butter with lots of seasoning. Nutmeg, cinnamon, mace, and minced parsley all taste good with rutabaga, and they combine well with carrots and parsnips. Alternatively, mash them after drying, season well, and serve as a rich purée. Cut into cubes or chunks, rutabaga adds flavor to soups, broths, and stews. They can also be roasted with a little oil and honey.

Rutabaga is rich in vitamin C, calcium and niacin.

In Ireland, the vegetable we call "turnip" is not a turnip at all but a rutabaga. Confusion regarding names is widespread, even with the introduction of small turnips and sweet-tasting *navets*, so different in appearance to the much larger rutabagas. In Scotland, the "bashed neeps" traditionally eaten with haggis are, in fact, rutabagas. However, there was a time about 300 years ago when there was only the turnip, for the rutabaga is a relative newcomer, a mid-European hybrid cross between a turnip and kohlrabi. In the 18th century it was grown in Sweden, then exported elsewhere in Europe where it is known as Swede, yellow turnip, or turnip-rooted cabbage.

Although similar to the turnip, the rutabaga is allowed to grow much larger so it has coarser skin, which can be quite knobbly. In shape, the rutabaga is round or slightly oblong, with a wrinkly neck made up of ridges, which are leaf scars. It is generally purplish brown in color with creamy yellow tinges, but some are yellow, purple, and

taro

Colocasia esculenta

Taro has a high starch content and is also rich in B vitamins. It has some vitamin C, potassium, and iron.

This tuber, which originated in East Asia thousands of years ago, is a staple food in tropical areas throughout the world, from China to Hawaii. There are about 200 varieties, which explains its many different names — eddo and dasheen are Caribbean, while keladi is Indonesian and Malay, and it is also known as cocoyam, colocassi, and elephant's ear. Those which you are most likely to encounter are the large, barrel-shaped tubers resembling rutabagas, and the smaller, potato-shaped tubers. These are dark brown in color and have a rough, shaggy skin. When buying taro, choose small, even-sized specimens, and store in a cool dark place, where they will keep for a few weeks.

Taro is often confused with the yam (yucca) but, unlike the yam, the bulbous taro has a ring of color at the base of the stem and all of the plant is eaten — the root, stem, shoots, and leaves. Taro also has a more distinctive flavor than the yam and has been described by some as rather like that of a water-chestnut. The tubers contain calcium oxalate below the skin — this is toxic and can only be eliminated by cooking. Therefore, when peeling taro, it is advisable to wear gloves as this prevents the toxins causing an allergic reaction. Taro can be boiled without peeling, the skin being removed after cooking.

Should you come across taro leaves (callaloo, a Caribbean speciality), these can be cooked in the same way as other leafy greens, but on no account should they be eaten raw because they too contain calcium oxalate.

Taro can be cooked in the same way as potatoes: boiled and mashed, roasted, fried, braised, or made into fritters. As it readily absorbs the flavors of other ingredients, it is well suited to making soups, stews, and casseroles.

A rich source of vitamin A, with significant amounts of B3, C, and E and small amounts of calcium, phosphorus, potassium, sodium, zinc, and iron. It is also a good source of fiber.

As a child I was told, along with probably every other child of my generation, that if I ate my carrots I would be able to see in the dark. I remember a visit to the movies, walking into the auditorium and groping for my seat in the dark. In no time at all I could see quite clearly, which I assumed was due to my obedience in not leaving a single carrot on my plate. It was quite a few years later when I learned that there was a scientific basis for the medical claims for carrots, and that World War II pilots were encouraged to eat them to help with night flying.

The original carrot of Asia Minor must have been very unimpressive. It is described by Nika Hazelton in her book *Vegetable Cookery* as "small, tough, pale-fleshed, and acrid", a far cry from the vibrant orange vegetable we know today. The Greeks and Romans certainly ate those early carrots, and prized them for their medicinal qualities, particularly for digestive ailments, but it was not until the coming of the Moors into Europe in the early Middle Ages that carrots appeared with any similarity to those of today, although the color was then purple. In fact, the familiar orange color is a Dutch invention of the late 18th century.

Carrots now come in numerous shapes, sizes and colors. Parisienne carrots are short, round and stubby, about 2 inches long and 1½ inches across, and slightly rusty orange in color. They have a sweet earthy flavor and a texture between a crisp carrot and a soft parsnip. More familiar varieties range from 5 inches long and ½ inch wide to 8 inches long, finishing in a pointed or blunt end. Across

the widest part they can be as much as 2 inches. When young, they are sweet and deep in flavor, they are crisp and succulent, and bright golden orange. These young carrots are often sold with their feathery leaves still attached (opposite page.) Special varieties of very small carrots, no bigger than a little finger, are also available. These are sweet and succulent. Carrots generally range from bright orange to a more muted orange–brown, but there are also varieties which have white, yellow, or purple roots.

Buy firm, smooth, well-shaped, even-sized carrots with a bright color. Small to medium carrots generally have a sweeter flavor and more refined texture than large varieties, which may have more depth to their taste, but are inclined to be woody.

Very small carrots are best served raw or very lightly cooked. When serving them as part of a raw vegetable platter selection, leave a little foliage on or trim off the foliage to leave about ¼ inch of stalk. The skin is so fine that it is not necessary to peel them, simply wash, scrub and dry. To cook very small carrots, steam or boil them in just enough water to cover for a few minutes until they are just tender and the water has evaporated. The delicate flavor of small carrots needs no more embellishment other than to be tossed in some melted butter and seasoned with salt, freshly ground black pepper and lots of minced flat leaf parsley.

Carrots that are 4–5 inches long with tender skin can also be scrubbed and washed. Most of the precious nutrients are stored just under the skin, so only peel very large or older carrots with skin that is more textured or damaged. Medium and large carrots need to be trimmed top and bottom, then they can be cut into slices, sticks or dice and boiled or steamed. They will take 8–20 minutes, depending on their size and age. Carrots are heat-sensitive and need to be steamed or boiled fast rather than simmered or they will never become tender. My favorite way is to just cover them with boiling water, add a lump of butter and a pinch of sugar, and boil over a high heat with the lid on the pan until almost tender. The lid is then removed and any remaining liquid reduced to a light syrup before adding lots of chopped parsley or chives, and plenty of salt and freshly ground black pepper. These are known as Vichy carrots. After simply steaming or boiling, carrots can also be drained, dried, and mashed, and they are good mashed with parsnips. They can also be made into a purée or mousse, or added to pancakes, desserts, and cakes.

Large carrots can be cut into large chunks, par-boiled until they are just beginning to tenderize, then drained and roasted around a joint. Alternatively, diced large carrots may be mixed with other diced root vegetables and roasted with a little honey. It is these carrots that add an earthy flavor and substantial texture to robust stews and casseroles, and are indispensable in soups.

Raw carrots are equally valuable grated or cut into julienne as a major ingredient in salads, in which they taste excellent with either a mayonnaise or vinaigrette dressing. They combine well with many other ingredients, including cabbage, peas, dried fruit and citrus fruit, nuts and mustard. Herbs that go well with carrots include coriander, dill, chervil, tarragon, and parsley; spices are nutmeg, cinnamon, caraway, coriander, turmeric, and cumin.

carrot
Daucus carota

High in carbohydrate and rich in potassium, with some folic acid, zinc and B vitamins.

The yam or yucca could easily be described as the potato of Asia, now widely cultivated as a staple in tropical regions and originally spread to Africa and the New World as a result of the slave trade. This is not the Louisiana yam which is a variety of sweet potato (see below.) There are numerous shapes, colors, and sizes, variously described as greater yams, water yams, sweet yams and Asiatic yams. Those that we see in the market are generally thick, oblong tubers with skin that is brown, rough and a little hairy. The skin can vary from white to pink, yellow and dark brown, depending on the variety, and in some cases can also be smooth. The color of the hard flesh can vary, from white right through to purple. As far as taste goes, yams are rather bland, but their ready availability and versatility attracts cooks around the world.

When buying yams, choose those with firm unbroken skin. They will keep for several weeks if stored in a cool, dark place.

The skin of the yam contains the poison dioscorine, but this is destroyed during cooking. Small young yams can be cooked in their skins, but larger yams are best peeled. To boil yams, first wash them, then cook them in a saucepan of salted boiling water for 10–20 minutes. Yams can also be baked in their skins, or peeled, then roasted or mashed. They can be cut into cubes or slices and added to casseroles and curries, and they are excellent cut into slices and deep-fried. In West Africa boiled yams are made into *fufu*, a kind of mush that is traditionally served with spicy stews and soups.

yam (yucca)
Dioscorea

Rich in carbohydrate, Jerusalem artichokes are high in iron, with moderate amounts of vitamins B and C.

A hardy native of North America, imported to Western Europe in the 17th century, this is a real ugly duckling among vegetables – small, knobby, and irregularly shaped. This is a shame, because it has a wonderful nutty flavor and a meltingly tender texture. The name Jerusalem artichoke is said to stem from the Italian *girasol articocco* — *girasol* meaning "toward the sun" and *articocco* because some people believe it has a smoky taste similar to that of the globe artichoke. Strangely, despite its name, it has nothing to do with Jerusalem.

When selecting Jerusalem artichokes, pick the least knobby you can find, so that preparation is less tedious. A new, straighter variety is becoming more widely available, and is worth seeking out.

Sadly, this winter vegetable has long been neglected and underestimated, mainly because it has a reputation for causing gas in some people — unfortunate but true. Handling and cooking is similar to that of the potato. Scrub artichokes well to remove any soil or grit, then wash them. If the skin is smooth and fairly blemish free, peeling is unnecessary, and since most of the nutrients lie just under the skin it is best left on. If the artichokes are peeled, sliced or diced, keep them in water to which the juice of half a lemon has been added. The acidulated water

Jerusalem artichoke
Helianthus tuberosus

helps to preserve their pale color, so too does adding a little milk to the water when boiling.

Jerusalem artichokes can be boiled or steamed, either whole, halved, quartered or sliced. I like their rugged appearance and cook them whole for 12–15 minutes until tender, then toss them in lots of butter and seasoning and sprinkle with chives or parsley. They also taste good tossed in a nut-flavored oil, which emphasizes their own nutty flavor. To roast them, peel, par-boil for 8–10 minutes, then drain and roast in hot fat or oil until crisp and golden – just as you would potatoes.

Fried Jerusalem artichokes are equally tasty. Par-boil or par-steam them, then slice and fry in oil and butter. They are delicious mixed with strips of fried bacon and chopped herbs. They can also be dipped in flour, egg and crumbs or batter and deep-fried. When sliced very thinly and deep-fried, they make excellent crisps. Sliced cooked artichokes make tasty gratins with cream, herbs and cheese, and boiled artichokes can be mashed to a purée. They can be used to make soup, and eaten raw, grated and tossed into a salad with a little lemon juice or vinaigrette. They are also good cooked and sliced or diced in salads.

sweet potato
Ipomoea batatas

Rich in carbohydrate, beta carotene and vitamin C with moderate amounts of potassium.

Although this vegetable has the same name as our own favorite vegetable, it is from a completely different plant, a member of the morning glory family. While some varieties look similar to our potato, most do not, and the overriding flavor characteristic is sweetness.

Originally from the humid regions of the Americas, probably the Andes, it was discovered by the Spanish in the 15th century and brought to Europe. However, it was never established outside the warmest regions because of its growing characteristics. There are many different varieties and many different names – kumara, ubi, keledek, ubi manis and Louisiana yam to name just a handful.

The skin can be smooth or rough textured, and ranges in color across a wide spectrum from white through to pinkish purple and deep brown. The flesh also has a great variety of color: white, cream, yellow and bright orange among others. The texture varies from dry and mealy with a flavor reminiscent of chestnuts, to waxy.

Sweet potatoes can be prepared and cooked just like potatoes: boiled, mashed, sautéed, baked, roasted, and fried. They can be boiled with or without their skins, but take care when cooking them in their skins as they are more delicate than the ordinary potato. They will discolor quickly after peeling and should be put into acidulated water. They make good soups and stews because of their distinctive flavor and ability to combine well with other ingredients. Eastern spices and flavors like lime, coconut milk, ginger, and coriander (cilantro) marry well with sweet potatoes. Because of their sweetness, they are also widely used for sweet tarts, pies, and pancakes.

parsnip
Pastinaca sativa

Parsnip has moderate amounts of vitamins A and E, small amounts of C and B, with some iron, calcium, phosphorus, and potassium. It is high in carbohydrates.

Parsnips are thought to have originated as wild plants in Asia Minor, but there seems to be no evidence that the ancient Egyptians or the Greeks used them, though they seem to have been well established by Roman times. It appears that they spread through the northern parts of the Roman Empire into Gaul and Britain, where ideal winter growing conditions produced the characteristic sweetness caused by the conversion of starch into sugar. The old traditions of using crushed parsnips for making jam, desserts, and fermented drinks like parsnip wine seem to date from the Roman period.

Parsnips are the edible underground roots of a plant related to parsley, fennel, celery, and carrots. Some are stocky and bulbous, with slightly humped shoulders and an inverted leaf core, and some are more wedge-shaped with wide shoulders and a long root. Others have the wedge shape but are much longer and narrower from top to tail. There are also dainty miniature versions.

You can grow parsnips in your own garden. For cooking, select medium-sized roots, firm and well-shaped. Avoid very large parsnips as they may be fibrous and woody. The younger the better, and the less preparation needed. If they are from the garden, cut the leaves off and discard, then scrub the parsnips under cold running water. Medium and large parsnips need the skin scraped or peeled with a vegetable peeler if they are coarse. Small and miniature parsnips have fine skin, and so need little or no peeling. Large parsnips need the woody core cut out: cut them in half or quarters lengthwise, then cut out the core. Parsnips can be cut into chunks, slices, lengths, finger strips, or dice; they can also be left whole if they are no more than 3 inches long and fairly narrow. Steam or boil them until just tender, for 10–20 minutes, then toss in butter or cream and season well. To roast parsnips, halve or quarter the thick end and leave the pointed sections whole. Cover them with cold water, bring to a boil and cook for 1 minute. Drain, then add to hot fat and roast for about 30 minutes. Parsnips make good French fries, left as they are or dipped in batter, deep-fried or sautéed in butter and oil. In Ireland, one of the most popular ways of serving them is boiled and mashed with carrots, plenty of butter, salt, and pepper. They can also be mashed with potatoes, and made into fritters, cakes, and soufflés. Parsnips are delicious in robust winter stews. Their sweetness goes well with curry spices, parsley, chives, nutmeg, and cinnamon.

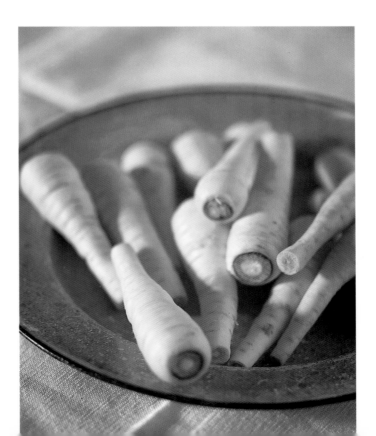

radish
Raphanus sativus

High water content, moderate amounts of vitamin C with some calcium and iron. It has a little protein and is also low in calories.

The radish is an ancient food, favored by the pyramid building Egyptian slave workers, the Greeks, and the Romans, and recognized for its diuretic and cleansing properties since earliest times. In Britain it has been eaten as a salad vegetable for well over 1,000 years.

While the radish with which we are most familiar is small, with a deep reddish-pink skin, firm white flesh, and neat vibrant green leaves, there are in fact many other varieties. Some are slightly more oblong in shape and blushed with white at their tip, these are known as the French breakfast radish, and have a more delicate taste than the standard red varieties like Cherry Belle and Scarlet Globe. Other varieties in this group may be pink, yellow, or purple in color, and either round or cylindrical in shape. These radishes are best eaten young and raw, either on their own with salt (they are good with drinks), in salads or as part of a raw vegetable platter. There is also a variety of radish known as the winter, Chinese, or Spanish radish. This has white flesh and a skin color that can range from black to purple, white and red. Its shape can also vary, from small and round to elongated, and it can weigh 1 pound and over. One type of winter radish is the black radish (below left.) It is large with firm, compact flesh. These kinds of radishes are eaten raw, either sliced or grated and used in salads, but they can also be boiled like turnip, made into soup, and added to casseroles and curries.

Daikon (below right) This large white Japanese or oriental radish, also known as daikon, is impressively long and about 2 inches in diameter with smooth skin. It generally has a mild flavor and is extremely popular in oriental cuisine, raw, cooked and pickled. It has a very crisp, juicy texture and is often served finely sliced or shredded raw as an accompaniment or garnish for Japanese foods. It also adds interest to soups and stir-fries.

High in carbohydrates and low in fat. A good source of vitamin C with some vitamin B. A high mineral content with magnesium, potassium, iron, calcium, phosphorus, and sodium.

The Irish didn't invent the potato, although it was once termed the Irish potato to distinguish it from the sweet potato. The potato has its origins in the high Andean plateaus of South America some 5,000 years ago. It was a staple of the Inca nation and was not discovered by Europeans until the time of the Conquistadors in the 16th century. Returning adventurers, including Francis Drake, brought the potato to Europe, but it was slow to catch on. It was the Irish who first grew it as their principal staple crop then, as emigrants, introduced it into North America in the early 18th century.

There are some 400 varieties of potato. Their cooking characteristics are dependent on the amount of water they contain. Floury potatoes are soft and break up easily, so are good for mashing, fluffy roast potatoes, and French fries. Waxy potatoes are firmer and keep their shape better; they are best for boiling (when they are to be served whole) and for using in salads. Potatoes are affected by light and turn green quite quickly, so store them in the cool and dark, but not the refrigerator because the extreme cold converts the starch into sugar.

Nutrients are contained in and just below the potato skin, so scrape or peel very finely, only if necessary. Alternatively, cook potatoes in their skins and peel after cooking if necessary. This is particularly suited to cooked potatoes for salads.

To boil potatoes, ensure they are of even size, or cut them into even-sized pieces. Cook, covered in boiling water, but don't boil too fiercely or the potatoes will break up. Timing depends on size and variety, but is generally 15–20 minutes. Steaming is more gentle and good for potatoes which tend to break up. Timing is 15–20 minutes. To bake, prick the skins with a fork and bake in a preheated 400 degree oven for 1½ hours. To roast, peel and cut into even-sized pieces, rounding off sharp edges. Put into a saucepan of fast-boiling water, return to a boil, and

cook for 10 minutes. Drain, return to the saucepan to dry, and shake to roughen the surfaces. Place in a roasting pan with a little hot oil or fat and toss to coat. Roast in a preheated 400 degree oven for 40–50 minutes, turning and basting several times. To sauté, slice cooked potatoes and fry in a large heavy pan in a little hot oil for 15–20 minutes. To deep-fry, peel, and cut into fries. Dry well, then gently lower into a pan of deep fat, preheated to 325 degrees. Cook for 8–10 minutes, until crisp and golden brown. Drain well before serving.

potato
Solanum tuberosum

podded vegetables

High in vitamin C with moderate amounts of vitamin B. Also contains calcium, iron, potassium, and trace elements.

Okra originated in North Africa, and possibly Egypt. It is thought to have spread to the Middle East, where it is known as *bahmia*, and then to India, where it flourishes in the sub-tropical south and is known as *bhindi*. It was introduced into the Caribbean and the Deep South around the 17th century. Robbed of their homeland and identity, slaves carried with them into bondage the seeds of familiar plants — okra being one of them. A by-product of this period in history is that okra became an important ingredient in Creole cooking.

Also known as ladies' fingers and gumbo, okra is the fruit pod of a tropical plant, five-sided, elongated and slightly pointed in shape. It looks a little like a lantern with a conical cap, an elegant lady's finger, hence its alternative name. Okra is dull green in color with slightly hairy skin and rows of tiny seeds inside the pod. The unique quality of okra is the mucilaginous substance which exudes when the pod is cut or exposed to heat during long slow cooking. This last characteristic is particularly useful for thickening soups and stews and is perfectly illustrated in the Creole dish called gumbo, a cross between a soup and a stew with a thick, gluey consistency. Gumbos are now the hallmark of Creole cooking.

Always buy small, young, crisp pods — mature okra is fibrous. The ideal length is about 2–3½ inches. Scrub the pods well under cold running water, then trim off the stalks. If you are going to use the okra whole, leave the conical caps on and carefully pare around them to neaten their appearance, otherwise slice the okra, cutting off the caps with the stalks. When very young, small and tender, okra can be eaten raw in salads, either whole or sliced, otherwise they need to be cooked.

Boil or steam okra for 8–10 minutes until just tender. Drain, then toss in butter, season with salt and pepper and serve as an accompaniment. Okra has a particular affinity with garlic, lemon or lime juice, and corn. It also goes well with Spicy Tomato Sauce (page 232.) Fry whole okra in a little butter or oil for a few minutes, add the tomato sauce, and cook gently for 20–30 minutes until the okra is tender. Season well, then sprinkle with minced flat leaf parsley and serve hot with pita bread, or cold with plain yogurt and finely chopped mint.

Frying whole okra seems to prevent them becoming slimy. Heat a few tablespoons of oil in a skillet, add a little garlic and chili powder, and fry until soft but not colored. Add the whole okra and toss for 1–2 minutes until just tender, a few minutes more if you prefer them to be crisper. Remove the okra from the pan with a slotted spoon, set aside to drain on paper towels. Serve as a snack or as a side-dish with curry. For a slightly crunchy texture, whole okra can be tossed in flour, beaten egg, and cornmeal, and fried in about 1 inch of vegetable oil. Whole or sliced okra can be added to any type of soup or stew. The taste of okra marries well with chicken, ham, bacon, lamb, shrimp, tomatoes, onions, garlic, chili peppers, bell peppers, ginger, and Indian spices — it really is a truly versatile vegetable.

okra
Hibiscus esculentus

green bean

Phaseolus coccineus

High in protein, carbohydrate and fiber. Moderate amounts of vitamins C and A, beta-carotene and iron.

The green bean is one of the many New World beans, a native of Central America and thought to have been a food crop for over 2,000 years. The "scarlet runner," a climbing green bean, was introduced into Britain in the early 17th century as an ornamental plant, grown for its pretty scarlet flowers and delicate leaves around gazebos, arbors and arches, over trellises and walkways, as well as in flower beds. It was also used in posies and bouquets. It was not until the end of the 19th century that the green bean began to be used as a vegetable, but its wonderful flavor was soon recognized and it became an important feature in cottage gardens throughout the country.

Green beans are long and flat with a slightly rough skin and purple seeds within the pods. To best enjoy their distinctive fresh flavor, eat them when they are in season from July to October. They are at their best when small, young and tender. For this, you need to grow your own, or have a friendly gardening neighbor. Unfortunately, it is rare to see small green beans in the shops, and frozen varieties can be bland and wilted. At their best, green beans should be firm and snap easily. To be sure of this, they should be picked just before cooking.

To prepare green beans, wash and dry them, then top and tail. Many of today's varieties are stringless, but check for any strings and remove if necessary. If the beans are thin, short and young, they can be eaten raw in salads, either whole or sliced. They can also be stir-fried, steamed or boiled until tender, allowing 5–7 minutes, then drained and tossed in melted butter or olive oil and a dash of balsamic vinegar. Larger beans can be cut into thin, elongated diagonal pieces and treated the same way. Sometimes I toss cooked green beans with a light sesame oil and lemon juice, or I finish them with a few tablespoons of heavy cream, along with plenty of seasoning and minced parsley. Or I make a thick spicy tomato sauce and either cook the beans in it or toss them in it just before serving. Sometimes I use a pepper sauce instead. Another favorite way is to stir boiled green beans into a mixture of thinly sliced fried onions, garlic and chanterelles with plenty of seasoning, chopped parsley and a dash of balsamic vinegar.

French green bean

Phaseolus vulgaris

Rich in protein, carbohydrate, vitamins B and C. Also includes potassium, folic acid, beta-carotene, and high amounts of the essential amino acid lysine.

The French green bean, a native of South and Central America, was introduced into Europe by the Conquistadors in the 16th century. Also known as bobby bean, Kenyan bean, string bean, green bean, dwarf bean, haricot vert, haricot bean, wax (yellow) bean and Thai bean, it is one of many beans that are native to the New World.

The beans can be flat, oval or round in shape, and range from 2½–3 inches to 9 inches in length and ¼–½ inch across. Their skin and flesh may be green, yellow, purple, or marbled, and their seeds are colorful or mottled. They are grown for their immature pods, which are eaten whole with the tiny seeds still inside. Once they ripen and mature, they are dried, and the seeds are then eaten as navy or great northern beans. Perfect winter nourishment.

Look for fleshy beans, irrelevant of their shape or color. They should be firm, crisp, and snap easily (hence another of their names). The preparation and cooking of all varieties is the same. Wash and dry, then top and tail. If the pods are very large, cut them in half or into 1½ inch lengths.

French green beans taste so fresh and distinctive that they require little embellishment. Their crunchy texture is good in a vegetable platter or salad of mixed leaves or crisp vegetables. The taste and color are preserved with quick cooking such as stir-frying in a little oil for a few minutes, on their own, with garlic or with other vegetables. They can also be steamed or boiled in the minimum amount of water for as short a time as possible. Cook for 5–7 minutes, just until tender, but do not cover the pan or the beans will lose their bright green color. Drain, return to the pan, and toss with a little butter or olive oil. Season well before serving, and add a splash of herb vinegar. This family of beans also marries well with fried onions and a seasoning of minced parsley and thyme. For a more substantial dish, they can be cooked in a well-flavored tomato sauce. If you have an excess of French beans, they can be added to a mixed vegetable soup.

High in protein, carbohydrate, vitamins B and E, potassium, calcium, and phosphorus.

The culinary history of the pea is an ancient one. Pea seeds have been found in the tombs of ancient Egypt, and certainly the Romans cultivated them. The dried pea was a major source of protein throughout the Dark Ages and into Medieval times, but it was not until the 16th century that we find the first references to the green pea.

The garden pea is harvested from the end of May, and it is at this time, and for several months, that fresh peas are sold in their pods. When they are plump, small, and bright green they are tender and sweet with an incomparable flavor. If they have been allowed to get big and their pods a little wrinkly, they are not worth eating, and frozen peas are a better choice. If you grow your own, pick them just before you need them, and either eat them raw or cook them immediately after shelling. Raw peas taste great in a mixed leaf salad.

To boil peas once shelled, put them in a saucepan and cover with about 1 inch of boiling water. Add a sprig of fresh mint. Return to a boil, cover with a lid and cook until just tender, 3–5 minutes. Drain and top with a lump of butter and a few chopped mint leaves, or return the peas to the pan, and toss with a little thick cream and seasoning to make a light sauce. For me, there is only one other way to serve fresh peas and that is *"à la française"*,

pea
Pisum sativum

combining two summer vegetables which flourish at the same time — lettuce and peas. Finely shred several small lettuce hearts, put them in a heavy casserole dish and add a few finely chopped spring onions, about 1 pound of freshly shelled peas, a lump of butter, and a little water. Cover the casserole dish with a piece of nonstick baking paper and the lid and cook for about 20 minutes. By this time the peas will be tender, the lettuce wilted and most of the liquid evaporated. Season well and serve immediately.

Fresh garden peas make an excellent addition to a meat or vegetable stew, added about 5 minutes before serving. Puréed, they make a wonderful soup or sauce for poached chicken or fish, or the base for a soufflé. When cooked, they can be stirred into quiche fillings, omelets, and rice dishes such as risotto, or into a white sauce with cooked ham and chicken to make a savory tart or pie filling. Topped and tailed fresh young pods can be boiled and tossed with melted butter, or used to make a soup or purée, either on their own or combined with shelled peas.

Snowpeas and Sugar Snap peas

These are also members of the Pisum sativum family. They have a similar appearance to the garden pea, but the snowpea has a much flatter pod, which tapers at both ends and is about 3 inches long and ½ inch across. The tiny peas (seeds) are just visible through their almost translucent pod. The entire pod is eaten, accounting for its French name, which means "eat all." Like sugar snaps, snowpeas have a wonderful crunchy texture. The sugar snap pea, also known as sugar pea, is fatter, and falls somewhere between the garden pea and the snowpea. Its flavor is more pronounced and sweeter than that of the snowpea, tasting more like a raw garden pea, but it is also eaten in the pod like the snowpea.

When choosing snowpeas or sugar snap peas, look for crisp pods which have a bright green, juicy appearance. Some are sold ready topped and tailed, but if not, simply cut a little off each end and remove the string from along the edge.

Both snowpeas and sugar snap peas can be eaten raw, allowing you to enjoy their fresh taste and crisp texture. Use them whole with other vegetables in a plate of raw vegetables, sliced in a mixed green leaf salad, or sliced and combined with garden peas, celery and some other crisp vegetables, lightly moistened with vinaigrette. Orange goes well with snowpeas, so sometimes I include some orange segments in a salad and sharpen the vinaigrette with orange juice.

To cook these peas, either boil or steam them as quickly as possible to preserve their texture and color, about 3–5 minutes. They should be only just tender, with no hint of sogginess. Drain and toss quickly in melted butter. They cool down very quickly, so serve immediately, piping hot. You can toss them with chopped fried bacon, fresh herbs, and salt and pepper, or stir-fry them with other vegetables, either whole or sliced lengthways along the diagonal. Cook them very quickly, adding them almost at the end of cooking, just to warm through and combine with the other ingredients. Both snowpeas and sugar snap peas make excellent soup.

High in protein, carbohydrate and fiber. A good source of calcium, potassium and iron, also vitamins A, B, C, and E.

Also called broad beans and horse beans, fava beans are one of the first vegetables of the spring, appearing in May and June. Their season is very short, so be sure not to miss them. They have rich green, velvety pods that can grow to over 12 inches in length, but when they reach this size are only good for soups, purées, and stews.

They are at their sweetest and most tender when no longer than 3–4 inches. Both seeds and pods should be bright green. The best way to have a ready supply is to grow them, because they are not often seen like this in the shops. Pick or buy them just before use because the pods go limp very quickly after picking, the sweetness diminishes and the texture alters. The fava bean is one of the least altered by freezing, so either pick them and freeze them immediately or buy commercially frozen beans – both are very good.

Very young, small beans can be eaten whole. Wash, dry and top and tail, then serve them raw as part of a raw vegetable selection, dressed with a light garlic vinaigrette, or with cured ham, salami or cheese. To cook fava beans, either boil them in the minimum amount of water or steam them for 4–5 minutes until tender, then drain, season and serve with melted butter, or toss in a little thick cream which has been reduced by boiling.

fava bean
Vicia faba

As the pods get larger, shell the beans and either serve them raw in salads, or cook and serve them as for the young pods. The French add a little savory to the boiling water and scatter some of the chopped herb over the beans before serving. Cooked fava beans combine well with spices such as chili, nutmeg, and cinnamon, and with garlic, zucchini, tomatoes, green onions (scallions), celery, other beans, ham, bacon, chicken, and cured meats.

For luxurious service, drain the beans after cooking, cool slightly under cold water, then slit the skins and squeeze the beans out. Toss the succulent jewels in warm butter, cream or sauce and serve hot, or toss in a light vinaigrette and serve cold or use in salads. This is the perfect treatment for older beans. When young, the whole pods can be cut into pieces between the beans and braised with flavoring vegetables, pork, bacon, or smoked beef.

corn
Zea mays

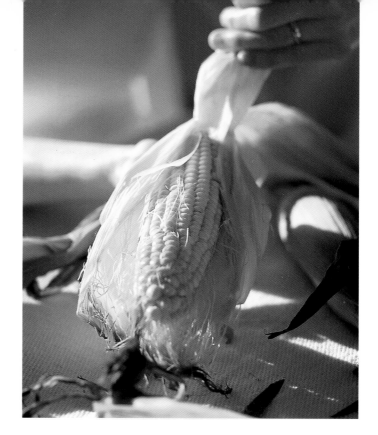

High in carbohydrate and fiber, corn is rich in vitamins A, C and some B. It also contains potassium, magnesium sulfur and iron.

Maize, or corn as it is better known, is the third most important cereal in the world, with a history of cultivation stretching back to its origins as an edible grass in the Andean foothills. It was revered as the core of life in the golden civilizations of the Americas — the Inca, the Maya and the Aztec — and was a staple of the indigenous tribes of North America. Discovered by Columbus, it was brought to Europe and used mainly as cattle fodder. It is only recently that corn has been eaten as a vegetable.

From the moment the corn cob is picked, the natural sugars change into starch, causing a loss of sweetness. So use them as soon as you get home or, if you grow your own, pluck and cook them immediately. Corn should have bright green husks that snuggle around the kernels. The silk at the end of the husk should appear feathery and be turning dark brown at the tip. The kernels should be tightly packed, plump, and juicy. Baby corn, which is picked when still immature, should look lively and creamy yellow, with juicy kernels.

Corn-on-the-cob To boil, strip off the husks and silks, then rinse the cobs. Cook in fast-boiling unsalted water for 7–10 minutes until the kernels are tender. Test frequently after 7 minutes, taking care not to overcook. Drain and serve with butter and seasoning.

To grill, strip off the husks and silks, or leave the husks on and strip out the silks. Soak the cobs in cold water for at least 30 minutes, then drain and pat dry. If the husks have been removed, brush the kernels with a little oil. Grill on the barbecue for 15–20 minutes, turning frequently. The cobs can be cut into chunks, ½–1 inch thick, soaked, then skewered, and grilled in the same way.

To roast, prepare as for grilling, then wrap in thick foil. Roast in the hot coals of a barbecue or on a baking sheet in a preheated 400 degree oven for 20–30 minutes. Oven roasting can be done without aluminum foil; simply brush the cobs with a little oil.

Whole baby corn are best eaten raw with a dip or light sauce or mixed into salads. I sometimes stir-fry them, which retains their qualities better than boiling.

Corn kernels Remove the husks and silks from raw cobs, then wash and dry. Scrape the kernels off with a sharp knife, then drop the kernels into fast-boiling water and scrape the cob over the pan to squeeze out the milky juices. Cover and cook for 3–5 minutes. Drain, toss in butter or cream and season well. The kernels can also be boiled in milk or cream. They can be added to soups and stews, used in fritters, pancakes, omelets, frittatas, and salads, and used in fillings for pies or tarts.

fruiting vegetables

Rich source of vitamin C. Also contains vitamins A, B1, B2, and E, and small amounts of potassium and folic acid. Excellent source of fiber.

There are certain objects which I am drawn to, attracted by color, shape, and texture. The urge to touch and to pick up is irresistible, the feel in my palm and against my fingers a sensual pleasure. There is a vegetable which fulfills this sense more than any other — the bell pepper or sweet pepper, whose vibrant colors remind me so much of early childhood and my first bright paints. Peppers are a vital ingredient in much of my cooking, one of a quintet of ingredients for healthy, Mediterranean-style eating — olive oil, garlic, tomatoes, bell peppers, and red wine.

Poor old Columbus. In 1492 he didn't succeed in his objective to discover a sea route to the fabulous Orient, nor did he perchance discover the American mainland. He returned to his Spanish patrons with no gold, no precious stones and no silks. Instead he brought back evidence of the rich plant life he had discovered, amongst which were members of the capsicum family — sweet peppers and their kinsmen, chili peppers.

Peppers are positively bursting with color — yellow, orange, red, green, deep violet-purple, and black. Their flavor varies slightly, depending on the color. The green pepper, although mature, has been picked rather than being left to ripen on the bush. It has a slightly sharper, more savory, flavor than the red pepper, which is fully ripe with sweet-tasting flesh. The yellows and oranges are also

pepper

Capsicum annuum

more sweet than savory, but not as rich or mellow as the deep, almost ruby-red varieties. The white, black and violet-purples are more akin to green peppers in taste.

The most common peppers are bell-shaped, hence one of their names 'bell pepper' (another is bullnose pepper). They have 3–4 lobes, which widen slightly towards the stalk end and are then pulled into the centre of the hollow fruit, creating slightly humped shoulders. Some peppers are long, tapered and pointed, others short and wide or heart-shaped.

Peppers should be firm and very smooth, with a bright glossy sheen. They should have thick flesh and feel heavy. The green stalks should still be intact, an indication of freshness. They first need to be washed or wiped, then dried. If the pepper is to be sliced in strips or diced, it can be cut in half lengthways and the stalk, pith, core and seeds pulled or cut out, along with any tough membrane. If you are going to cut the pepper into rings or stuff it whole, cut around the stalk to release it from the flesh, then pull it out along with the seeds and core. Then turn the empty shell upside down and tap it on the work surface to dislodge any remaining seeds.

If the pepper is to be roasted or broiled whole, leave the seeds, core, and stalk intact and remove them after cooking. This gives the pepper more flavor because it cooks in its own juices in a sealed parcel. If the pepper is to be roasted or broiled after being cut in half, remove the seeds, core and stalk before cooking.

Roasting and peeling sweet peppers alters the whole appearance and structure of the vegetable, reducing any sharpness to a rich softness. In the case of red peppers, it gives them a concentrated sweetness, almost as though they have had sugar added. Lightly rub the whole pepper with oil, then put in a heavy roasting pan or dish and roast in a preheated 425 degree oven for 30–40 minutes until the skin is blistered and charred black in places. This charring gives a smoky flavor to the flesh. Alternatively, the pepper can be impaled on a heavy metal skewer with a wooden handle and roasted over an open gas flame until it blisters and softens. This is quicker than the oven method, but it requires constant turning for 10–15 minutes. The skin can also be charred and blistered under a fierce broiler, over a barbecue, or among the hot ashes or coals of a barbecue or open fire. Once the peppers are cool enough to handle, the skin should peel away easily.

If you have a problem, seal them in a plastic bag for about 10 minutes, then remove them and peel the skin away. Cut the peppers in half and remove the seeds along with the core and any pulpy ribs. Some people wash the seeds out, but I don't like to lose any of the precious juices or wash the flavor away.

Roasted and peeled peppers can be sliced or diced. My favorite way is to cut them into wedges or thick strips and marinate them in olive oil, garlic, parsley, thyme and savory for a few days before serving in a salad with olives and anchovies, or rolling them up, securing with skewers and serving with drinks. They are also delicious stirred through lightly cooked egg dishes, such as omelets or scrambled eggs, or mixed with fried onions and used to fill pies and tarts. They can also be used as a base for dishes like Goat's Cheese with Peppers & Pine Nuts (page 135).

Sliced or diced raw or roasted peppers can be fried in olive oil and served as an accompaniment, added to stews and braised dishes and used in dishes such as ratatouille, peperonata, piperade, soups, sauces, and purées.

Because of their shape, peppers make ideal containers for stuffing, served raw or cooked. Remove the stalk, core and seeds by cutting out at the stalk end, or cut off a slice containing the stalk to make a lid and remove the core and seeds from it. The vegetable can then be stuffed and baked if required. If baking, drop the pepper into boiling water for 1 minute, then drain and refresh before stuffing. This keeps the taste sweet and shortens the oven cooking time.

An excellent source of vitamins A and E.

Chili peppers are members of the capsicum family. They bring color, fire, and zest to cooking, and kick even the blandest foods into life. There are literally hundreds of varieties. Some are small and round like cherries, others are shaped more like sweet peppers, but are smaller and puffier like little bonnets. Some are long, thin, tapering cones, while others are slightly fuller, wrinkly, and stubby. In color, they range from green through yellow to red.

The heat-producing element in chilies is a volatile oil called capsaicin. It is measured in Scoville units, which range from 0 for sweet peppers to over 300,000 for the habañero. A medium-hot chili pepper is around 600 units. Capsaicin is concentrated in the seeds and white parts, so these need to be removed unless you want to add excessive fire to your dish. This volatile oil has a burning effect on the skin and eyes, so when handling chilies, take care not to rub your eyes or touch your face or mouth.

Add chili peppers gradually to your cooking to get the degree of heat you want. Generally, the smaller the chili, the more fiery, likewise the dark green chili peppers, and those that are thin and sharply pointed. Ancho chilis look similar to sweet peppers, but are much smaller. They are relatively mild, with an underlying sweetness. Anaheim are longer than ancho, about 4 inches, thin and with a rather blunt end. They are red or green, generally with a mild,

chili pepper
Capsicum frutescens

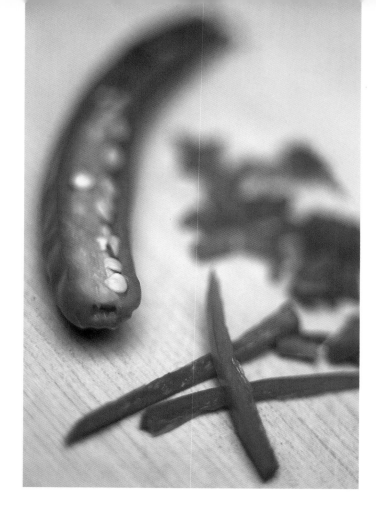

sweet taste. Jalapeño, probably the best known chili, are quite short and blunt. They start dark green and eventually turn red. Chipotle are smoked jalapeño. Bird's eye or bird chilis, also known as Thai or pequin chilis, are small and pointed, red, orange, green, or cream, and very hot. Serrano are Spanish chilis that are small and thin. Red or green, they can be mild or hot. Poblano chilis are small and dark green. They generally have a mild, spicy flavor, but may also be scorching hot, it is hard to tell. In Spain they are eaten in tapas bars, either roasted or broiled whole. They are also widely used in Mexican dishes. Habañero are pretty, like tiny, shiny, sweet peppers, but their appearance is deceptive — they are the hottest peppers in the world. Scotch bonnets are cousins of the habañero chili.

Chili peppers add spice, heat, and a distinctive flavor to otherwise bland ingredients such as rice, beans, and lentils. They can be added to meat and vegetable stews, poultry and fish, and are extensively used in soups and sauces. Some varieties are even stuffed and eaten whole.

cucumber
Cucumis sativus

Mostly water, but a good source of potassium and some vitamins A and C.

The cucumber's wild forebear is many thousands of years old with origins in Asia. It was favored by the Greeks and Romans, eaten cooked and raw for its high water content and refreshing effect, even though it was considered to be indigestible and the cause of excessive gas. Even today, this characteristic causes some people to avoid it.

The classic British cucumber is 12 inches long and green, about 1½ inches in diameter and with a slightly ridged skin, but the variety most often found in the United States is shorter, more squat, and has a yellower skin. When buying cucumbers, ensure they are firm, bright in color, and unblemished. Cucumber is generally considered to be a salad vegetable to be eaten raw. It is generally sliced thinly into rounds for salads, but it can be chopped or shredded, as it is for many Middle Eastern dishes and the Indian side dish Cucumber & Mint Raita (page 216), in which it is mixed with yogurt and served with curries for its cooling effect. It is the main ingredient in the chilled Spanish soup gazpacho, and makes a refreshing cold or iced soup in its own right. When cooked and combined with cream, herbs and spices, cucumber is delicious, and goes particularly well with fish dishes. It is seldom that anyone has afternoon tea these days, so the cucumber sandwich belongs to a bygone age, kept alive only in fancy hotels, and sometimes taken on summer picnics.

Good source of vitamin A, with some C and small amounts of B. Small quantities of folic acid, potassium, and iron.

The pumpkin's name derives from *pepen*, the Greek word for melon. It was brought to Europe after the discovery of the Americas by European adventurers, and was soon established as a bulking substance in stews and soups.

Pumpkins grow to some size, up to 60 pounds. I find the best between 7–11 pounds, no bigger than a beach ball. Some pumpkins are more oblong than round and the skin color ranges from warm buff to bright orange and even gray. The skin can be smooth, rough, or ribbed. The flesh is usually orange, with a mild, sweetish flavor.

Select pumpkins that are clean, heavy, and bright. They should sound hollow when rapped with the knuckles. The skin should be thick and firm, free from bruises and cracks. If buying wedges or halves, make sure the flesh is moist and well wrapped. Pumpkins improve with keeping; the flavor concentrates and they are said to have "cured." They will keep for months in a cool, dry place. Once cut, cover the exposed surface and store in the refrigerator for up to two weeks. The flesh can also be puréed and frozen.

Pumpkin skin is very hard and inedible and needs to be removed if raw flesh is required. Cut the pumpkin into wedges like a melon, then remove the seeds and fibers. Saw off the skin from each piece, then cut the flesh according to recipe requirements. Like this, the pumpkin can be boiled or steamed until tender, drained, and tossed in butter. It is particularly good seasoned with ground cumin and coriander, garlic, or ginger. It can be used to make soups and stews, baked with cream, cheese, and spices to create gratins, and roasted in large chunks. It can be used in risottos, or dipped in batter and deep-fried.

Pumpkin can also be baked. Cut it in half across the widest part and pull out the seeds and fibers. Score the flesh, taking care not to pierce the skin. Rub the pumpkin with oil and lay each half, cut-side down, in a roasting pan. Cover loosely with aluminum foil and cook in a preheated 400 degree oven for 1–2 hours or until the flesh is tender. When cool enough to handle, dice the flesh or purée it.

pumpkin
Cucurbita maxima

zucchini
Cucurbita pepo

Reasonable source of vitamins A and C, with small amounts of calcium and potassium. Low in calories.

Zucchini are simply baby squash. The history of the zucchini is similar to that of other members of the squash or gourd family. Zucchini were introduced to Europe from North America during the 19th century. They are classified as summer squash and belong to the gourd section of that family.

Delicacy and size are important and small really is beautiful, 3–8 inches in length and ½–2 inches across. Look also for tiny "baby" zucchini no wider than ¼ inch and 2–2½ inches long. The most common zucchini has deep green skin with faint ribbing. The yellow zucchini is slightly straighter than the green, and the Italian zucchini is very long, thin, and pale lime green. You can also find round and bulbous varieties of zucchini. The skin should be brightly colored and glossy, thin, and smooth. The color, texture, and flavor of the flesh is the same in all varieties.

Zucchini require just a quick wash and wipe dry and trimming top and bottom. To cook whole baby zucchini, blanch them in boiling water for 10 seconds, then drain and toss with melted butter and perhaps a little softened garlic for a few minutes. If they are no more than 4 inches long, they can be cut into thin rounds or matchsticks and eaten raw in a salad or tossed in vinaigrette. They can also be grated, or very thinly sliced lengthwise to serve in a vegetable carpaccio. Medium-sized zucchini 4–6 inches long can be sliced across in rings of any thickness or cut on the diagonal, then tossed in butter, and served with lemon juice and seasoning. They can be cooked in a rich tomato sauce, added to ratatouille or moussaka, or baked with butter, rosemary, cream, and egg in a gratin. Strips or sticks can be stir-fried or broiled. Grated or diced zucchini can be used in omelets, risottos, vegetable mixtures, or scrambled eggs, or puréed to make a sauce or soufflé. They can also be coated in batter or egg and bread crumbs, and deep-fried. Larger zucchini can be hollowed out, stuffed, and baked in the oven.

squash blossoms

The wonderfully shaped, yellow-orange flower heads of zucchini and all other squash are edible, and can be used in both salads and cooked dishes. They do not keep well, and need to be used soon after picking. Wash them well and gently shake dry. They can be added to salads as they are, shredded and stirred into an omelet or scrambled eggs, or used to garnish soup. They can also be stuffed.

large zucchini squash

Cucurbita pepo

Composed mainly of water, marrow has some carbohydrate and few calories. It contains small amounts of minerals and vitamins A and C.

Large zucchini squash is one of the family of gourds, all of which are native to the Americas. This type is particularly popular in the United Kingdom, although it has only been eaten there since the middle of the 19th century.

The best-tasting large zucchini squash are no more than 12 inches long, with a firm feel, but still a little "give" when pressed with the thumb. They should be rounded with a glossy, bright, unblemished skin.

Large zucchini squash makes reasonable soup when combined with well-flavored broth and strong-tasting vegetables such as carrots and turnips, as well as herbs or oriental spices to give them a lift. The same applies if you want to use them for making preserves or chutney, which is one of the best ways of using large zucchini squash. The squash can be cooked with garlic, chili powder, red and green bell peppers, stem ginger, apples, and dried fruits.

To prepare large zucchini squash, wipe the skin, top and tail, then cut in half lengthwise. Remove the seeds and white parts, cut off the skin, then slice the flesh.

To cook large zucchini squash, cut the flesh into ½ inch dice, blanch in boiling water for 1–2 minutes, then drain and pat dry. Toss in a skillet in a little butter or olive oil with a hint of garlic until lightly browned. Serve with grated Parmesan cheese, or layer in a gratin dish with Parmesan and Swiss cheese, nutmeg, and minced parsley.

Cover with heavy cream and bake briefly in the oven.

I like to stuff and bake large zucchini squash. The stuffing needs to be well flavored, spicy, and highly seasoned. Add a touch of sweet pepper sauce or tabasco to make the mixture taste more lively. Rice will help to absorb the moisture in the squash, and a rich tomato sauce served with baked large zucchini squash is very tasty.

To prepare rings, cut the squash across into 1½ inch slices. Remove the seeds and white parts, leaving a cavity for the stuffing. To make boat-shapes, cut the squash in half lengthwise. Scoop out the seeds and white parts, then remove the remaining flesh to form a boat with 1 inch thick walls. Chop the flesh and mix it with the other stuffing ingredients. Blanch in boiling water for 3–4 minutes, drain and pat dry. Set it in a lightly oiled roasting pan. Pack the rings tightly together and pile stuffing in the cavity, heaping it up so that it will soak up the juices from the squash. Put 2–3 tablespoons water or stock around the summer squash, dot the stuffing with butter and cover with foil. Bake in a preheated oven, 200°C (400°F), Gas Mark 6 for ¾–1 hour.

squash
Cucurbita pepo

Squash have a high water content, with varying amounts of vitamins A, B and C, and minerals. They are low in calories.

The squash family is of New World origin. The word squash comes from the native American *askutasquash*, which means "eaten raw." Whether or not this is how they were first tasted by the Pilgrim Fathers when they were coming to terms with the bleak reality of survival in the early 17th century is not sure, but those harsh early days are now commemorated each November in the traditional Thanksgiving dinner. The pumpkin has an honored place at the table, along with the turkey and cranberries.

Squash are classified according to season as either summer or winter squash. Summer squash are best eaten fresh and young before the seeds have had time to develop, while winter squash are allowed to mature on the plant to be harvested in the fall so they have thicker, harder skins than their summer cousins and the flesh is more fibrous. They benefit from being stored in the light and warmth for a few weeks after harvesting to "cure."

Shades of green, soft creams, honeys, harvest russets, empire suns, and sunset reds demand exciting flavors to complement such color. Enrichment with butter, cream, or olive oil is a starting point. Mingling with savory flavors like garlic, herbs, spices, and strongly flavored cheese is transforming. For dessert, ingredients such as cinnamon, nutmeg, sugar, honey, and ginger are a delight. In general, squashes can be baked, boiled, roasted, steamed, or fried. They are ideal for stuffing, make excellent purées, and are delicious in warming soups and stews. They can also be pickled, made into chutneys or deli cious preserves and, to round off the menu, can be transformed into a range of desserts from the traditional pumpkin pie to mousses and compotes, and used as a flavoring for breads and cakes.

1-inch dice and add to a saucepan of boiling water. Bring back to a boil, then simmer for 5–6 minutes. Kabocha squash can also be roasted. Cut the flesh into 2–inch dice, baste in hot fat and roast in a preheated 400 degree oven for 40–50 minutes.

Acorn squash (opposite page, right) A small heart-shaped winter squash, similar to a large acorn. Acorn squash have ridged beautiful deep green or orange skin, or a mixture of both, and firm, bright orange flesh. Like pumpkin, acorn squash can be peeled, wrapped in aluminum foil and baked. I like it diced, tossed in butter and served with cheese. It also makes wonderful soup.

Butternut (page 80) A winter squash resembling a giant pear with a hard, buttery colored skin. It has deep orange flesh, which is firm, nutty and slightly sweet. It is excellent for soup or any pumpkin recipe. Baking really seems to concentrate its flavor.

Crookneck Named after its awkwardly shaped neck, this summer squash is bright yellow-gold in color and is best used when it is about 4 inches long. Prepare it as you would Pattypan. Or cut it in half lengthwise, brush with butter, and sprinkle with cheese, then bake in a hot oven for 10–15 minutes.

Hubbard As can be seen from its other names of golden hubbard and blue hubbard, this winter squash has a wide range of possible colors from bright orange through yellow to blue. It is large and has a thick hard shell with a bumpy texture. The flesh is slightly grainy, particularly when the squash is very large. Hubbard are best boiled or roasted and prepared like pumpkin.

Kabocha squash (opposite page, left) Originating from New Zealand, this attractively colored squash makes an ideal accompaniment to any meal either boiled or mashed. It has a firm texture and is full of flavor. To boil, first peel and remove the seeds, then cut the flesh into

Little gem (page 89, back right) This winter squash is small, round, and dark green. When picked, it looks like a baby watermelon, the size of a tennis ball. As it matures it turns a rich yellow color. Its flesh is pale yellow and has a delicate nutty flavor. Boil or steam whole for about 20 minutes. Cut in half, remove the seeds, and serve with butter and freshly milled black pepper. It mixes well with other ingredients, such as garlic, onions, and tomatoes.

Onion squash This handsome winter specimen is bright reddish-orange in color, round, and onion shaped. It has a close texture and mild honey flavor that is not unlike pumpkin. It can be used for most pumpkin recipes.

Pattypan (page 89, front left) Also known as custard summer squash and scallop squash, this attractive summer squash is small and dainty with a fine skin in a variety of delicate colors: pale cream, green, and crocus yellow. Pattypan are almost round, but look as if they have been slightly squashed to form a curved, heavily scalloped edge. They have an elegant green stalk protruding from one end and a little top-knot on the other. In flavor they are very similar to zucchini and can be used in the same way — sliced across and fried in butter and oil, with a hint of garlic. They can also be steamed whole (this will take about 20 minutes), the top cut off, and a little of the center scooped out and filled with melted butter and plenty of seasoning. Prepared this way, an even greater portion of the flesh can be removed and added to a light savory stuffing of herbs, cream, and mild cheese. They can also be used to make soups, soufflés, fritters, and gratins. For best results, buy when the skin is tender and the specimen is no larger than 4 inches across.

Spaghetti squash A most unusual summer squash that has earned its name from the resemblance of its cooked flesh to spaghetti. It is also called vegetable spaghetti, spaghetti zucchini squash and noodle squash. The flavor is quite different to pasta, though. It looks rather like a summer squash and has the same ability to grow to an enormous size, but it is best no more than 8–10 inches long and around 2–2½ pounds in weight. It ranges from pale creamy white through varying shades of yellow and sometimes has a greenish tinge. It has a very distinctive fragrant flavor, and is at its best when boiled or steamed and served with butter, pepper, a little chopped garlic or green onions (scallions), a tomato or pesto sauce, and perhaps some Parmesan cheese. It can also be baked.

To cook, pierce the end with a skewer, then boil, steam or bake whole for 30–45 minutes. Drain, then cut in half lengthwise. Remove the seeds and then the flesh, using a fork to comb the spaghetti-like strands out of the shell.

Turk's turban This is one of the most beautiful of all the squashes. It is a winter squash, multi-colored, shaded and striped, deep orange, yellow, cream and green in varying hues. It looks like a small pumpkin with a smaller one pressed halfway into the center. Hence the reference to turban, because that is what it looks like. It has a firm yellow flesh and a nutty taste. It can be stuffed and baked.

tomato

Lycopersicon esculentum

Rich in vitamins A and C, with some vitamin B and some potassium and folic acid. High in fiber.

One bright morning, our neighbor arrived with a bag of baby tomatoes — all golds, reds, and greens — fresh from the greenhouse. We didn't wait until lunch, but ate them like the fruits they are with slices of mango and papaya for breakfast, sitting outside in the early September sunshine. The sea was a deep Mediterranean blue, the yachts were rocking gently in the harbor — and those pop-in-the-mouth, sun-ripened tomatoes tasted as tomatoes should, sweet and juicy with just a hint of sharpness.

The tomato is a colorful member of the nightshade family, in company with the potato, eggplant, pepper, and tobacco. Its origins can be traced back to South America and the Andean foothills before the time of Christ. By the time the Conquistadors arrived in the 16th century, tomatoes (*tomatl* to the Aztecs) had spread throughout Central America into Mexico and the north. The first tomatoes were yellow, and they received a very cautious reception in Europe, especially in the north, where the plants only became popular as a trailing decoration in gardens. The early Italian name was *pomo d'oro* (golden apple), which the French corrupted to *pomme d'amour* (love apple), and for a time the fruit was thought to be an aphrodisiac. Tomatoes were first introduced widely into Spanish and Italian cooking during the 17th and 18th centuries, but were not universally popular in Europe and the United States until the 19th century.

The tomato is the fruit of a vine, a berry fruit, which has pulpy flesh and seeds rather than stones. It can be bright pillar-box red, vibrant yellow, orange-gold, acid green, or striped variants of these. It may be round, oval, plum or pear shaped, and it can be big, up to 2 pounds in weight and over 4 inches in diameter, or tiny like a cherry, no more than 1 inch across. Its delicate juicy flesh can be red, blush pink, orange, or pale gold, and the flavor at its best is a perfect balance of sweetness and acidity. Home-grown tomatoes, sun-ripened on the vine and picked just after the sun has been on them, have the best flavor.

Salad tomatoes are the standard commercial crop available all year. They are about 2 inches round, orange-red and fairly juicy, with plenty of seeds and no particularly distinctive taste. This is because they are generally picked and ripened off the plant, which affects their flavor, but this can be improved by seasoning with salt, pepper, a pinch of sugar, and a little herb vinegar. Some of the most flavorsome are Ailsa Craig, Alicante, and Moneymaker. Vine-ripened tomatoes still attached to the stalk have an excellent flavor. They are deep red and slightly smaller than the common round tomato.

Cherry tomatoes are grown for their concentrated sweet flavor and dainty size. They are available in a choice of red or yellow, round, oval, plum or pear shapes. Some of the best are Tiny Tim, Phyra, Cherry Belle, Gardener's Delight, and Sweet 100.

Large or beefsteak tomatoes can be up to 2½ inches tall and 4 inches in diameter. They are pulled in slightly to the center where the stalk sits rather like the top of an indented beret. The skin is ridged and deep red or orange. The flesh is solid and substantial with only a few seeds. The flavor is generally reasonable and can be very good if they have been ripened in the sun. Some of the best include

Super Beefsteak, Delicious, Dombello, Marmande, and Oxheart Giant.

Plum tomatoes are richly flavored, fleshy Italian tomatoes with lots of juice, few seeds, and a rich red color. They need plenty of sun to ripen and develop their flavor. For growing, the best variety is Roma VF.

Sun-dried tomatoes have been dried in the sun or the light for several weeks until they have curled up and lost their moisture but none of their flavor. They can be bought in their natural dry state or preserved in oil. The flavor is very concentrated.

Choose tomatoes with a bright color and firm unblemished skin. I like to buy them with the calyx attached. If the tomatoes are not fully ripe, set them in a bright, warm, sunny place to ripen (or put them in a brown paper bag)

before storing them in the refrigerator. Remember to return to room temperature to recapture their flavor before use. If you want to freeze them, it is best to make them into a sauce, purée, or soup. Because of their high water content, whole tomatoes break down on freezing and cannot be used later for slicing or salads.

Before using tomatoes, wash and wipe them dry. If using raw, cut across their width into thick or thin slices. This is particularly appropriate if they are going to be served with slices of cheese such as mozzarella and dressed with a light vinaigrette. In some salad combinations they are best cut lengthwise, then into quarters or wedges. Sometimes they need to be skinned, seeded, and finely diced, especially for use in dishes such as scrambled eggs, omelets, and stuffings. When skinned, they are used in soups, sauces, and purées. Tomatoes are excellent in stews and casseroles particularly when combined with other sun-drenched vegetables like eggplant, zucchini, and peppers. Their acidic taste combines well with starchy vegetables like potatoes, dried beans, and chickpeas (garbanzo beans), and they are enhanced by fragrant herbs such as sweet basil, oregano, marjoram, thyme, rosemary, and bay leaf. Tomatoes taste good peeled and sliced, dipped in beaten egg and bread crumbs or cornmeal mush and shallow-fried, or cut in half, topped with butter, herbs, garlic and toasted crumbs, and broiled. They can be stuffed and served cold, or baked in the oven. Beefsteak tomatoes are just right for this treatment and make a perfect meal on their own.

A good source of vitamins C and A and high in potassium, with some iron, calcium, and magnesium.

Whenever I see this odd-looking vegetable, it puts me in mind of some heavily camouflaged tropical lizard waiting in the undergrowth for its prey. The skin is warty and changes color as the fruit matures — from silver-white to rich deep green then vibrant orange-red. It is a member of the bitter gourd family, a fruiting vegetable that grows on a vine. Bitter gourd, bitter cucumber, balsam pear, African cucumber, and karela are all related. Originally from tropical Asia, it is very popular in Chinese and Indian cooking because of its characteristic bitter flavor.

The fruits are generally picked young and small to avoid excess bitterness. When they are more mature, remove any extreme harshness by cutting the flesh or scraping the skin, then salting it. The bitterness can also be lessened by chopping it into cubes and blanching in salted water before use. Remove the seeds and central spongy section of mature fruit before cutting it into cubes or slices.

Chinese bitter melons are used in soups, curries, stir-fries, and other oriental dishes, as well as being stuffed with meat, fish, onions, and spices.

Kantola This is another bitter gourd, widely used in Indian and oriental cooking. Like Chinese bitter melons, kantolas need salting or blanching before use to remove any bitterness, then they can be sautéed or deep-fried, or added to stir-fries or curries.

Chinese bitter melon
Momordica charantia

avocado

Persea americana

An excellent source of vitamins A, C, B, and E. Particularly rich in potassium and magnesium, phosphorus, calcium, and iron. A good source of protein and fiber. It is cholesterol-free, low in sodium, and easily digested.

Avocado has long been enjoyed for its buttery, creamy flesh and the easy way it mixes with other flavors. Now we know that it is one of the most complete foods we can eat, packed with a unique combination of nutrients.

This sub-tropical berry fruit has been a staple in Central America for many centuries. It was prized by the Mayans and the Aztecs. Despite wide planting throughout Central America, it was not until the early 20th century that the avocado was first planted in California, but now it is established right across the globe, as far afield as South Africa, Australia, around the Mediterranean, and especially Israel.

There are four main varieties. Hass are medium to small in size, with a distinctive pear shape and a rough dark skin. Fuerte are medium-sized with an elongated shape and a rich green, slightly roughened skin. Ettinger tends to be larger than the other varieties, with a smooth and shiny thin green skin. Bacon has a smoky flavor.

All varieties have a large pit in the middle of delicately colored pale green flesh, and they all have a gentle, slightly nutty flavor. They are hardly ever "just ripe" for eating when bought, but will soon ripen in the warmth of a kitchen. The perfect avocado should yield slightly when gently pressed with a finger and thumb. An important point to remember is that the flesh discolors very quickly when cut. To help prevent discoloration, rub or toss all cut surfaces with lemon juice.

Cut the avocado in half down the center through to the pit, twist the two halves apart, and remove the pit. Fill the cavities with a dressing such as vinaigrette, or with something more substantial such as chopped fish or seafood. Diced avocado is good in salads, sandwiches, and salsas, while mashed avocado is the main constituent of the creamy Mexican dip guacamole.

The chayote is ninety percent water, so it is low in calories, though it contains some vitamin C and trace elements.

Toward the end of last year, some very good friends went to southeast Asia and Australia. Knowing they were about to have many exotic gastronomic experiences, I asked them to take note of the unusual vegetables and fruit they came across. One of the vegetables which struck them as peculiar was called *labu siam*. They described it as looking like a pear with ridges along the skin. Traveling on to the sub-tropical region in North Australia, they came across the same vegetable, this time called *choko*. The

description caused me to recognize it by the name chayote, familiar from the Portobello Road market in London, where it is sold imported from the West Indies. Chayote has many other names, including vegetable pear, chocho, chow-chow, christophene, chaka, mirliton, and pepinello.

This vegetable is a type of gourd. It originated in sub-tropical Central America, its most common name chayote being a corruption of the Aztec word, *chaytol*. Like many plants from this region, it now flourishes in hot and humid regions around the world. The vegetable grows on a vine, and in the humid growing conditions of the subtropics, the rate of growth is phenomenal. Although the ridged green skin form is the most common variety of chayote, there are others, including some with spiny, smooth, and even white, skins. I am always reminded of the avocado, with its different skin textures depending on variety. The chayote is bland, almost nondescript in flavor. It has a firm and juicy flesh, rather like that of a summer squash, which lends itself to many different cooking methods and flavorings.

Chayote is best eaten young and small. When very young, it is excellent raw, either diced or sliced in salads, in much the same way as cucumber is used. Young chayote can also be cooked whole, skin and all, like small zucchini. It works well in combination with tomatoes and strong flavors like bell peppers, chili peppers, garlic, and curry spices. As the fruit gets larger, it is best stuffed and baked like its cousin the summer squash, or used to make stews, curries and chutneys. In Caribbean and Central American cookery the chayote is a well-known ingredient in desserts, sweet tarts, pies, and cakes. I am told that in Mexican cuisine it is often used to add extra bulk to an apple pie.

chayote
Sechium edule

eggplant
Solanum melongena

Low in calories and rich in vitamins B and C, eggplant provides small amounts of iron and calcium.

A member of the nightshade family, the eggplant is actually a berry fruit, grown on a bush. It has a very long pedigree, having been eaten in India over 5,000 years ago. Its main migration was westward into the Middle East, although it was grown 2,000 years ago in China and there has been a long tradition of eating certain varieties in Thailand and Japan. From the Middle East it spread into Spain, Italy, around the Northern Mediterranean, and to North Africa.

The best-known eggplant is the long plum eggplant, slightly oval in shape. This variety is stunningly beautiful, with its purple-black, lustrous skin, so glossy it looks like it has been waxed. It is generally 6–6½ inches long and is topped with a green calyx and stalk, which remind me of an elf's cap. There are also miniature sizes (above right), which can be char-broiled, or halved, stuffed, and baked. There are many other shapes and colors — lilac-purple with creamy white marbling, purple-maroon, white, and white-green, as well as the plump ivory-white eggplant looking like large oval eggs (hence the name.) The Japanese or Asian eggplant is straight, long, and narrow. It ranges in color from a variegated lilac-purple and white to solid purple. Thai eggplant are often small and round (the tiny ones are called pea eggplant.) Some are dark green, some cream and green, others oval and golden yellow.

Eggplant should feel heavy and be firm but supple. The skin should be smooth with a high gloss. Pick small to medium eggplant as the flavor will be milder than that of larger specimens. After slicing or dicing, some people believe it necessary to draw out the bitter juices from eggplant flesh by sprinkling it with salt and leaving it to degorge before rinsing and drying. After years of experience I find degorging makes little difference to the flavor or amount of oil absorbed when frying, and it does nothing to improve the texture.

Eggplant absorbs any flavor which is added to them. Their texture is substantial and gives depth and distinction to mixed stews like ratatouille, caponata, and moussaka. They combine well with tomatoes, peppers and chili peppers, but they need to be cooked to absorb these flavors. To do this they can be fried, broiled, stewed, or baked, but avoid boiling, poaching, or steaming, as they will absorb the water like a sponge. Eggplant can be cut into slices about ½ inch thick and coated in batter or egg and bread crumbs and deep-fried, or cut into slices, spheres, or cubes to be fried in oil and served hot.

mushrooms

cultivated mushrooms

Cultivated mushrooms contain essential minerals, potassium, iron, sulfur, magnesium, and phosphorus. They are low in calories and are a great source of B vitamins and vegetable protein.

Mystique surrounds the mushroom. Its reputed magical powers, elusiveness, and the fact that some are poisonous — even deadly — have always made them fascinating. The Romans made special serving-dishes for them. The French were first to cultivate mushrooms in Europe from the beginning of the 18th century but the Chinese and Japanese were many centuries ahead of them, in their cultivation of shiitake mushrooms.

All mushrooms, whether wild or store-bought, should look fresh, have a clear bright color, and a dry texture. They should also be clean. Store them in the refrigerator in a paper bag (a plastic bag will make them sweat and become soft) where they should keep fresh for a few days.

Mushrooms are pretty full of moisture so they should not be soaked in water. A wipe with a damp cloth should be enough by way of preparation. Trim tough stalk ends if applicable and slice stalks and large caps for ease of cooking. Peeling should hardly ever be necessary.

The textures and flavors of different mushrooms are a delight. Some have a very subtle flavor, while others enjoy a more noticeable aromatic quality which can add depth of flavor to even the most simple of dishes. They are so versatile and can be prepared in a variety of ways. I find that the best way to cook mushrooms is by frying or sautéing in a little butter or olive oil, or a mixture of the two. They can also be dipped in batter or egg and bread crumbs, and deep-fried. Large mushrooms can be broiled or baked in the oven, with or without a stuffing.

stronger flavor is required. They are also good in pasta sauces, casseroles, and stews flavored with onions, garlic, tomatoes, and herbs. They keep their shape well.

Oyster mushroom (Pleurotus ostreatus, page 98) This mushroom can be found in the wild, growing on rotten elm logs, but it is now also widely cultivated and so available in supermarkets. It looks rubbery, and the stalk, gills and cap are all the same color, ranging from pinkish-brown to gray. Oyster mushrooms have a good flavor and a soft, silky texture, which makes them a welcome change from ordinary white and button mushrooms. They are best eaten when young. They have a high water content, however, so care is needed when cooking them, especially in combination with other ingredients. They taste good in stir-fries and have a special affinity with garlic.

Shiitake mushroom (Lentinellus edodes, opposite page). A variety of tree-growing mushroom originally from China and Japan, the shiitake is now widely cultivated and easy to obtain at supermarkets (although quite expensive). It is dark brown in color, with a rich meaty flavor and robust texture, ideally suited to vegetarian casseroles, stews and oriental stir-fries. Dried mushrooms sold in oriental shops are almost always shiitake, although they may not be labeled as such. See Dried Mushrooms (page 103.)

White and button mushrooms (Agaricus bisporus) These are by far the most common cultivated mushrooms, accounting for 60 percent of the world's production. Consequently, they are available throughout the year. They are sold at three stages of development: small (button), mid-size (closed cap), and large (open cap). Although fairly bland, they absorb other flavors well. They provide good bulk in stews and are excellent for soups and sauces where their flavor can be enhanced. They can be stewed, broiled or fried, and are good raw in salads, either sliced or whole.

Chestnut mushroom (Agaricus brunescens, above) With thick stems and brown caps, these have a little more flavor and a meatier texture than their white cousins. Use them in place of white mushrooms, in dishes where a

Wild mushrooms contain essential minerals, potassium, iron, sulfur, magnesium, and phosphorus. Low in calories, they are a source of B vitamins and vegetable protein.

Only pick your own wild mushrooms if you are absolutely sure of their identity and safety before using. All wild mushrooms should be brushed or dusted before storing, or dried for storage and used later. Any leftovers are much too valuable to waste, so slice them and dry them on a cookie sheet or threaded on strings. Choose a warm, well-ventilated place such as a shady porch or furnace room and leave them for a couple of days, or in the oven on the lowest setting for a couple of hours.

Cep (Boletus edulis) This handsome, fat-stemmed mushroom has a cream color and a bun-like cap. It is called *porcini* in Italy, and is renowned for its sheer versatility. It is at home in soups, sauces, stews and stuffings and is very frequently dried (opposite page.) When young, it can be eaten raw, and makes a flavorsome addition to a salad.

Chanterelle (Cantharellus cibarius, right) This firm-fleshed, curvaceous trumpet smells faintly of apricots. It is my favorite wild mushroom. Chanterelles range in color from cream to golden orange-yellow and keep both their color and texture when cooked. They are excellent in risottos, sauces, and egg dishes, and just a few will add a special flavor to the simplest dish. The ridges on the underside of the cap can trap dirt so they need careful cleaning. Dried chanterelles are a good substitute for fresh ones.

wild
mushrooms

Field mushroom (Agaricus campestris) This mushroom has a great deal more flavor than its cultivated cousin (Agaricus bisporus.) Its large white domed cap which later flattens is still a fairly common sight in fall fields. A good all-rounder, but I like it best when fried in butter or oil for a leisurely Sunday breakfast.

Giant puffball (Langermannia gigantea and Lycoperdon giganteum) It is always a great surprise when you come across this mushroom. It is a phenomenal size, as big as a beachball, with firm, white flesh. It is good to eat, fried or cut into strips and added for bulk to stews. One puffball is enough for several meals, but don't keep leftovers too long because they turn yellow and become inedible.

Horn of plenty (Craterellus cornucopioides) A little offputting in appearance because it is gray. In France they call it *trompette des morts* or "trumpet of the dead." I have occasionally found these mushrooms amongst chanterelles, which they resemble in shape. They go well with fish and white meats, and are a colorful contrast in white sauces.

Morel (Morchella esculenta and Morchella vulgaris) With its cone-shaped spongy top like a dark, pitted hollow cap, this mushroom looks rather like something picked up from a coral reef. It appears in spring rather than fall and is considered to be one of the great edible fungi. Morels need to be very carefully cleaned. Wash them under cold running water; no brush can get right into their tiny recesses.

Chicken of the woods (Hydnum repandum, below) Also called the hedgehog mushroom because of its spines, this mushroom does not have a particularly distinctive flavor, but it is relatively easy to find and it has a good, firm texture. It is best used in combination with other wild mushrooms, in egg dishes, especially scrambled eggs and omelets, risottos, and sauces for pasta. The spines underneath the cap are best removed before cooking.

Dried mushrooms

Many varieties of mushrooms are now widely available dried – cep, chanterelle, morel, and shiitake being the most common. Before using, cover with boiling water and soak for 15 minutes. Remove from the water and chop or slice as the recipe requires. The soaking liquid makes excellent broth, but strain it before use to make sure there is no grit or dirt from the mushrooms.

High in protein, mineral salts, potassium, and phosphorus, truffles also contain magnesium and calcium. Up to nine essential amino-acids have been detected in truffles. The nutritional value is higher than that of cultivated mushrooms, owing to a lower water content — ninety percent in mushrooms, seventy-five percent in truffles.

The truffle is the most sought after and most elusive of mushrooms, and therefore also the most expensive. It grows underground around the roots of trees (usually live-oak), hence the traditional need for dogs or pigs to sniff it out. The flavor is so powerful that even a very thin sliver or shaving is enough to transform the simplest of dishes. To prepare truffles, simply brush them gently with a vegetable brush to remove any grit, peel them if you like (the peelings can be used in soups, sauces and broths), then slice the truffle as thinly as you possibly can or finely shave it with a vegetable peeler. There are three edible varieties.

truffle

Black truffle (Tuber melanosporum, right) This is the most famous truffle from France, sometimes also called the Périgord truffle because it is found in the Périgord region in the south-west. It is a deep ebony black with a hard, knobby skin and can grow up to 5 inches in diameter, although most are 1–2 inches. Slivers or shavings of black truffle can be eaten raw, but they are more often used in cooking. They are good with eggs, in stuffings, braises and sauces (especially with Madeira), and they impart the most wonderful flavor to the flesh of chicken when inserted beneath the skin before roasting.

Summer truffle (Tuber aestivum) This truffle can be found growing in beech woods and is harvested in late summer, but unfortunately it is something of a rarity. It has a similar appearance to the white truffle (below), but has a wart-covered skin. The flesh is a solid brown color, with white veins running through. It can be used in the same way as white or black truffles.

White truffle (Tuber magnatum) Also sometimes called the Piedmont truffle, because it is exclusive to the Piedmont region in northern Italy. It is knobbly and like a potato in appearance. The skin and flesh range in color from cream to pale brown, and the flesh has a very firm texture. The white truffle has an exceptionally intense aroma and is the ultimate flavor prize. It can be added raw at the last moment, finely shaved or grated, to risottos, polenta, pasta, and egg dishes.

recipes

soups

chili, bean, & pepper soup

A fiery soup inspired by the rich colors and contrasting moods and flavors of Latin America. A devilish meal in itself, cooled by the subtle smoothness of an avocado salsa.

1 Heat the oil in a large saucepan and fry the onion and garlic until soft but not colored. Stir in the bell peppers and chili peppers and fry for a few minutes. Stir in the broth and tomato juice or passata, the tomato purée and paste, chili sauce, kidney beans, and coriander (cilantro.) Bring to a boil, cover and simmer for 30 minutes.

2 Cool slightly, then purée in a food processor or blender until smooth. Return to the pan and taste and adjust the seasoning, adding a little extra chili sauce if necessary. Bring to a boil and serve in warmed soup bowls, topped with avocado salsa and coriander (cilantro) sprigs and serve with lots of tortilla chips.

Serves 6

2 tablespoons sunflower oil

1 large onion, minced

4 garlic cloves, minced

2 red bell peppers, cored, seeded, and
   diced

2 red chili peppers, seeded and
   minced

3¾ cups vegetable broth

3 cups tomato juice or passata

1 tablespoon double concentrate
   tomato paste

1 tablespoon sun-dried tomato paste

2 tablespoons sweet chili sauce, or
   more to taste

1 x 13-ounce can red kidney beans,
   drained

2 tablespoons finely chopped
   coriander (cilantro)

salt and pepper

coriander (cilantro) sprigs, to garnish

To Serve:

Avocado Salsa (page 215)

tortilla chips

Chili Bean & Pepper Soup is shown on the preceding page

pumpkin soup
with crusty cheese topping

This substantial "eatin' and drinkin'" soup can be served in small hollowed-out pumpkin or squash shells. Indeed, pumpkin soup is an ideal way to use up the scooped-out flesh of a pumpkin, the result of making a festive lantern. Heat the shells in a very hot oven for about 10 minutes before using.

2 tablespoons sunflower or olive oil

1 large onion, minced

3 garlic cloves, crushed

2 celery sticks, chopped

3 cups pumpkin flesh, roughly chopped

3 cups light vegetable or chicken broth

pinch of freshly grated nutmeg

1 bay leaf

a few parsley stalks

⅓–⅔ cup heavy cream

1–2 tablespoons minced parsley

salt and pepper

To Garnish:

1 small French bread

½–¾ cup Swiss or fontina cheese, grated

4 flat leaf parsley sprigs

1 Heat the oil in a saucepan and fry the onion and garlic until soft but not colored. Add the celery and pumpkin flesh and fry for 10–15 minutes to draw out the flavors. Stir in the stock and nutmeg. Tie the bay leaf and parsley stalks together with string, add to the pan, and bring to a boil. Reduce the heat and simmer for about 30 minutes until the vegetables are soft.

2 Remove the bouquet of herbs and purée the soup by pushing it through a fine vegetable mill or puréeing in a blender. Return the purée to the saucepan, bring to a boil, and season with salt and pepper. Stir in the cream and parsley, return to a boil, then reduce the heat and keep the soup warm while preparing the garnish.

3 Cut the French bread into twelve ½ inch slices, place on a cookie sheet, and toast under a preheated broiler until pale golden on both sides. Leave the broiler on.

4 Pour the hot soup into 4 deep ovenproof bowls. Arrange 3 pieces of French bread on top of each one, overlapping them slightly. Sprinkle the soup generously with grated cheese. Set the bowls on the cookie sheet and brown quickly under the broiler until golden brown and bubbly. Garnish with parsley sprigs and serve immediately.

Serves 4

zucchini & dill soup

A flavorsome soup, perfect in the height of summer when there is a glut of zucchini. It is excellent served chilled and freezes well. Fresh dill gives a refreshing tang, but if it is not available, use fresh garden fennel or just a pinch of dried dill. For an entirely different flavor, use fresh basil leaves.

1 Heat the oil in a large saucepan and gently fry the onion and garlic until soft but not colored. Add the zucchini, cover tightly with parchment paper, and cook over a low heat for 10–15 minutes until tender. Add the broth, cover with a lid, and simmer for a further 10–15 minutes.

2 Using a slotted spoon, transfer the zucchini and a little of the broth to a food processor or blender. Purée until smooth, then pour into a clean saucepan. Add the remaining broth and the dill, season to taste with salt and pepper, then bring to a boil.

3 Serve in warmed soup bowls, each one garnished with a swirl of cream and fresh dill.

Serves 8

2–3 tablespoons sunflower or light
  olive oil
1 large onion, chopped
2 garlic cloves, crushed
4 cups zucchini, sliced or
  roughly chopped
5–6 cups vegetable or chicken broth
2–4 tablespoons minced dill
salt and pepper

To Garnish:
½ cup light cream
dill

beet borscht
with sour cream & chives

This vibrant, blood-red soup has a tangy, sweet-and-sour taste. There are many versions, ranging from a simple beet juice to a complex combination of meat and beet broth enriched with fresh and salted boiled beef, pork, and shredded cabbage. Traditionally finished with sour cream, borscht can also be accompanied by lavish helpings of fried sausage links, sliced boiled meats, small meat dumplings, and Piroshki (page 247). For many years I enjoyed this soup in the home of my friend Gran Kanareck, whose family were Polish. This is her recipe.

1 Scrape young beets, or peel older ones with a potato peeler, then grate the flesh on a coarse grater into a large saucepan. Grate the carrot and onion into the pan. Add the garlic, broth, lemon juice, and sugar and season with salt and pepper. Bring to a boil. Cover the pan, reduce the heat and simmer for 45 minutes.

2 While the soup is cooking, prepare the garnish. Cut the whole cooked beets into ⅛-inch slices, then into ⅛-inch sticks about 1½ inches long. Cover and refrigerate until required.

3 When the vegetables for the soup are tender, strain the contents of the pan through a sieve lined with cheesecloth. Discard the vegetables. At this stage the beet juice can be cooled and stored in the refrigerator until required. It will keep for several days. It can also be frozen.

4 Put the beet juice into a clean pan along with the beet sticks. Gently bring to a boil, then simmer for a few minutes to warm the beets through. Taste and adjust the seasoning as necessary, ladle into warmed soup bowls, and serve with a tablespoon of sour cream and a sprinkling of snipped chives.

Serves 6

CHEF'S TIP This soup can be thickened slightly with egg before adding the beet sticks. Lightly beat 2 eggs in a bowl. Whisking continually, pour a cup of hot (not boiling) beet juice on to the eggs. Pour this into the soup, whisking all the time to blend with the rest of the beet juice. Add the beet sticks and reheat very gently without boiling.

1½ pounds fresh raw beets, washed

1 carrot

1 onion

2 garlic cloves, crushed

1½ quarts well-flavored beef or vegetable broth

juice of 1 large lemon

2 tablespoons sugar

salt and pepper

To Garnish:

1 large cooked beet

⅔ cup sour cream

1 teaspoon snipped chives

gazpacho Andaluz

This cold, tomato-based vegetable soup, often referred to as "liquid salad", is one of the most refreshing of all summer soups. Originally from Andalucia in Spain, there are now many different versions. This is my "quick" recipe, which keeps well in the refrigerator for several days and also freezes well. If full-flavored fresh red tomatoes are not available, you will get a better color and taste by using canned chopped tomatoes — use three 13 ounce cans.

1 Reserve about 4 tablespoons each of the onion, bell peppers, and cucumber for the garnish. Put the remaining diced vegetables into a food processor or blender with the fresh and canned tomatoes, garlic, and tomato paste, and work to a smooth purée.

2 Add the tomato juice, water, sugar, oregano, and wine vinegar, then process again until well mixed. Season with salt and pepper. Transfer to a large bowl or pitcher, cover, and chill for at least 2 hours.

3 Just before serving, divide the reserved diced vegetables between 7–8 chilled soup plates, pour the cold soup on top and garnish with the garlic croûtons and snipped chives.

Serves 7–8

½ cup onion, finely diced

1 green bell pepper, seeded and finely diced

1 red bell pepper, seeded and finely diced

1½ cups cucumber, peeled and finely diced

3 cups well-flavored red tomatoes, peeled, seeded, and coarsely chopped

1 x 13-ounce can chopped plum tomatoes

3–4 garlic cloves, crushed

2–4 tablespoons double concentrate tomato paste

2 cups tomato juice

⅔–1¼ cups water

1–2 teaspoons soft brown sugar

1 teaspoon finely chopped oregano

5 tablespoons red wine vinegar

salt and pepper

To Garnish:

⅔ cup **Garlic Croûtons (page 249)**

1 tablespoon finely snipped chives

corn chowder

This is real comfort food, just the thing for a fireside supper on a cold wintry night. Chowder was originally a soupy stew from Brittany. It was taken to Newfoundland by the Breton fishermen, and then traveled down the Atlantic coast to New England.

1 Melt the butter in a large saucepan, add the onion and garlic, and fry over a gentle heat without coloring until soft. Add the diced potato and cook for a few minutes. Add the milk, sherry, and broth, season with salt and pepper, and bring to a boil. Reduce the heat to a simmer and cook for 10–15 minutes.

2 Add the corn, return to a boil, and simmer for 10–15 minutes. Meanwhile, prepare the sage garnish. Heat the vegetable oil in a deep-fryer to 425 degrees, drop in the sage leaves, and deep-fry for 20–30 seconds until crisp. Drain on paper towels and keep warm.

3 When the soup is ready, pour three-quarters of it into a food processor or blender and purée until smooth. Add the purée to the soup remaining in the pan and return to a boil.

4 Season with salt and pepper and stir in the cream and lime juice, adding a little extra broth if necessary to obtain the desired consistency. Heat the chowder thoroughly and stir in the chives. Serve immediately, garnished with the sage leaves and accompanied by cheese-flavored potato chips.

Serves 6

VARIATIONS Just before serving, add one or more of the following and heat through: thin strips of cooked chicken breast and roasted red bell pepper; diced green chili peppers; diced plum tomatoes.

Instead of the sage leaves, garnish with skinned and mashed roasted red bell pepper mixed with lightly whipped cream.

Roasted cumin seeds or hot spices, such as chili powder, cayenne pepper, and paprika, can be fried with the onion and stirred in before adding the broth or sprinkled on top of the finished chowder.

4 tablespoons butter

1 large onion, finely diced

3 garlic cloves, minced

½ cup potato, finely diced

1¼ cups milk

6 tablespoons medium sherry

2½ cups vegetable or chicken broth

3 cups fresh or frozen corn kernels or 2 x 11½ ounce cans corn kernels, drained

⅓ cup light cream

2 teaspoons lime juice

2 tablespoons snipped chives

salt and pepper

To Garnish:

vegetable oil, for deep-frying

12 sage leaves

Cheese-flavored Potato Chips (page 243)

celery & lovage soup
with herb cream & croûtons

Lovage is a herb with a flavor somewhat similar to celery, but much stronger. It is easy to grow and widely available in nurseries and garden centers in seed or plant form. Once established in the garden it is a prolific grower which can reach 2–6 feet in height. It is most attractive during the spring and summer, dies back in the fall and has vanished by winter, but sends out new shoots in the spring. If fresh lovage is not available, use 1 teaspoon crushed celery seeds instead.

1 Melt the butter in a large heavy saucepan. Add the celery, onion, leek, and potatoes, cover well with nonstick baking paper, and sweat over a gentle heat for 10–15 minutes until soft but not colored.

2 Stir in the lovage leaves and pour in the broth and milk. Season with salt and pepper and bring to a boil, then cover the pan and reduce the heat to a simmer. Cook for 20–25 minutes.

3 Purée the soup in batches in a food processor or blender until smooth. Return to the pan, adjust the seasoning and consistency as necessary, and bring to a boil.

4 Mix the cream with the chopped herbs, reserving a few. Pour the hot soup into warmed soup bowls, spoon a little herb cream on top of each one, and sprinkle with the reserved herbs, celery seeds, and croûtons.

Serves 6

4 tablespoons butter
3 cups celery sticks, chopped
1 large onion, roughly chopped
1 small leek, white part only, sliced
½ cup potatoes, cubed
14 large lovage leaves, chopped
3 cups vegetable or
  chicken broth
1¼ cups milk
salt and pepper

To Garnish:
⅔ cup heavy cream, lightly whipped
1 tablespoon each minced lovage,
  parsley, and chives
¼ teaspoon celery seeds
6 tablespoons Croûtons (page 249)

minted green pea soup
with hot paprika & croûtons

Green pea soup made with the first tender young peas of the season is one of the most delicious offerings from the spring vegetable garden. In this recipe I have combined them with the velvety leaves of mint, the sharp fresh flavor of lime, and the heat of paprika to produce a color and flavor which is hard to equal. If you are not able to get freshly picked garden peas, use good quality frozen petits pois. These produce a result which is equally good and can be enjoyed throughout the year.

1 Heat the oil in a large saucepan and fry the onion and celery until soft but not colored. Stir in the paprika and fry for a few minutes. Bring the broth to a boil in another saucepan and add to the pan with the peas, mint, and lime juice. Bring to a boil, then reduce the heat and simmer for 15–20 minutes until the peas are tender. If using frozen peas, cook for only 5–8 minutes. Don't overcook the peas or the soup will lose its bright green color.

2 When the peas are soft, blend the soup in a food processor or blender until smooth. If you prefer a very finely textured soup, pass the purée through a sieve or vegetable mill. Return the purée to the saucepan, bring to a boil and season to taste. Remove from the heat and stir in two-thirds of the cream or crème fraîche, then add a little extra broth, if necessary, to give the desired consistency. Warm through gently.

3 Serve the soup in shallow soup plates. Whip the remaining cream until it just holds its shape and add a spoonful of it or some crème fraîche to the center of each plate. Sprinkle a little paprika on top of the cream and finish with a sprig of mint. Serve the croûtons separately.

Serves 6

1 tablespoon olive or sunflower oil
1 onion, chopped
2 celery sticks, sliced
1–2 teaspoons hot paprika
3¾ cups vegetable or chicken broth
6 cups fresh or frozen peas
3 mint sprigs
juice of ½ lime
⅔ cup heavy cream or crème fraîche
salt and pepper

To Garnish:
a little hot paprika
6 small young mint sprigs
6 tablespoons Croûtons (page 249)

tomato & orange soup
with basil cream

A refreshing soup for a hot summer's day when tomatoes are sweet and ripe and basil heavily perfumed. If you want to make this soup at other times of year when fresh tomatoes have a less intense color and flavor, it is best to use four 13-ounce cans of plum tomatoes.

1 Heat the oil in a large saucepan and fry the onion and garlic until soft but not colored. Add the tomatoes along with their seeds and juice and stir in the tomato paste, broth, orange rind and juice, and basil. Bring to a boil, reduce the heat, then cover and simmer gently for 20–25 minutes until the vegetables are soft and pulpy.

2 Let the soup cool slightly, then purée in batches in a food processor or blender and push through a plastic sieve into a clean saucepan to remove the seeds. Season with salt, pepper, and a little sugar. This will help counteract the acidity of the tomatoes without actually making the soup sweet. Return the pan to the heat and bring to a boil, then add a little extra broth or tomato juice, if necessary, to achieve the desired consistency.

3 To serve, fold the chopped basil gently into the whipped cream. Pour the hot soup into warmed soup plates, spoon a little basil cream on each one, and top with tiny basil sprigs and orange julienne.

Serves 6

ORANGE JULIENNE With a vegetable peeler, remove a thin paring of rind from an orange. There should be very little white part with the rind. Cut the rind into very thin strips (julienne) and drop them into a pan of boiling water for 30 seconds. Drain and refresh under cold water. Drain again and pat dry.

2 tablespoons olive or sunflower oil
1 onion, roughly chopped
2 garlic cloves, crushed
4 pounds ripe tomatoes, peeled and chopped
2 tablespoons tomato paste
2 cups vegetable or chicken broth
grated rind of 1 large orange
6 tablespoons freshly squeezed orange juice
4 basil sprigs
1–2 teaspoons brown sugar
salt and pepper

To Garnish:
2–3 tablespoons finely chopped basil
⅔ cup heavy cream, lightly whipped
6 small basil sprigs
orange julienne (left)

creamed celery root
& Parmesan soup

Celery root makes a rich, well-flavored and creamy textured soup, and it is particularly good when combined with a strong cheese such as the Parmesan in this recipe. If you prefer, you can replace the Parmesan with ½ cup strong blue cheese and use snipped chives for the garnish instead of parsley. Alternatively, the cheese can be omitted altogether and the soup finished with a few drops of truffle oil and a sprinkle of toasted pine nuts. Although truffle oil is expensive, a little goes a long way and it adds a wonderful flavor.

1 Melt the butter in a large saucepan and fry the onion, garlic, and celery root over a gentle heat for 4–5 minutes to draw out the flavors without coloring. Add the broth and bring to a boil. Reduce the heat to a simmer, cover, and cook for 25–30 minutes until the celery root is tender.

2 Let the soup cool slightly, then blend in a food processor or blender, in batches, until smooth. Return the purée to the pan and add half of the cream and Parmesan. Reheat and simmer gently for a few minutes, stirring to blend.

3 To serve, whip the remaining cream until it just holds its shape. Put 1 tablespoon of the remaining Parmesan in the bottom of each warmed soup bowl and pour on the hot soup. Add a spoonful of whipped cream to each bowl and garnish with a grind of black pepper and a sprinkling of chopped parsley. Serve with the scones.

Serves 6–7

2 tablespoons butter
2 large onions, roughly chopped
I garlic clove, crushed
**1¾ pounds celery root, to give about
  I pound when peeled and
  roughly chopped**
5 cups vegetable or chicken broth
1¼ cups heavy cream
**4–8 tablespoons Parmesan cheese,
  freshly grated**
salt and pepper
**2 tablespoons finely chopped parsley,
  to garnish**
**Cheese, Leek & Herb Scones
  (page 240), to serve**

roasted pepper soup
with tomatoes, garlic, & fragrant herbs

Roasted vegetables of all varieties have a very distinctive flavor but the rich sweetness of charred red peppers is one of the most exquisite. The quantity of broth needed will vary depending on the amount of juice created by the vegetables during roasting. You may also need to add a little concentrated tomato juice if the fresh tomatoes are lacking in flavor. This soup is also excellent cold, when it should be garnished with thin strips of roasted red pepper and some freshly chopped herbs instead of the cream.

1 Put the oil into a large roasting pan, about 14 x 10 x 2½ inches, and heat on the top of the stove. Add the peppers, tomatoes, onions, carrots, celery, garlic, and chili peppers, and toss to mix. When they are sizzling hot, transfer to a preheated 400 degree oven, and cook for 1 hour, stirring occasionally. Remove the pan from the oven, stir in the tomato paste, and let the vegetables cool.

2 Transfer the vegetables to a food processor or blender and process until very smooth. This may need to be done in batches. Push through a plastic sieve into a clean saucepan to remove any remaining skin and seeds. The purée will be thick and rich with a brilliant orange-red color and a magnificent flavor. In this form, it can be used as a sauce or stirred into other vegetable dishes.

3 Put the thyme, basil, and parsley into the food processor or blender with about ⅔ cup of the purée and process until well blended. Add to the rest of the purée in the saucepan. Dilute with the vegetable broth to the desired consistency. Season with sugar, salt, and pepper and a little Tabasco sauce if you feel the need for a spicier chili flavor. Serve in warmed soup bowls, garnished with a spoonful of crème fraîche and a sprig of basil or parsley.

Serves 7–8

4 tablespoons olive oil

5 large red bell peppers, total weight 2–2½ pounds, cored, seeded, and roughly chopped

2 pounds red tomatoes, halved lengthwise

2 large onions, roughly chopped

2 carrots, roughly chopped

2 celery sticks, chopped

10 large garlic cloves, peeled

1–2 small red chili peppers, seeded and finely chopped

2 tablespoons double concentrate tomato paste

2 teaspoons finely chopped thyme

3 tablespoons finely shredded basil

2 tablespoons finely chopped flat leaf parsley

5–6 cups hot vegetable broth

1–2 teaspoons brown sugar, to taste

Tabasco sauce, to taste (optional)

salt and pepper

To Garnish:

1 cup crème fraîche

7–8 basil or flat leaf parsley sprigs

Jerusalem artichoke soup

This soup has an earthy, almost smoky, flavor and an attractive texture and color. Choose young artichokes that are not too misshapen and of a reasonable size — between 2–4 inches — so they can be used without peeling. If you don't want to make the fries for the garnish, use croûtons instead, or slivers of toasted almond.

1 Melt the butter in a large heavy saucepan and fry the onion, garlic, and celery gently until soft but not colored. Add the artichokes, then tightly cover the vegetables with a piece of parchment paper to "sweat" them and draw out their flavor. Cook over a low heat for 10 minutes.

2 Stir in the vinegar and flour, then gradually add the broth, stirring to blend all the ingredients together. Season lightly with salt and pepper. Bring to a boil, reduce the heat, then cover and simmer for about 30 minutes, or until the vegetables are tender.

3 Let the soup cool slightly, then purée in a food processor or blender until smooth. Return to the pan and bring to a boil. Adjust the seasoning, stir in the cream, and reheat the soup thoroughly. Add a little extra cream or broth , if necessary, to achieve the desired consistency. Serve hot, garnished with artichoke fries, minced parsley, and parsley sprigs.

Serves 9–10

6 tablespoons butter
1 large onion, minced
2 garlic cloves, crushed
4 sticks celery, roughly sliced
2 pounds Jerusalem artichokes, well scrubbed and sliced
1 teaspoon white wine vinegar
1 tablespoon all-purpose flour
1½ quarts vegetable or chicken broth
about ¾ cup light cream
salt and pepper

To Garnish:
Jerusalem Artichoke Fries (page 248)
2 tablespoons minced flat leaf parsley
flat leaf parsley sprigs

appetizers

vegetable carpaccio
with Parmesan shavings

This vegetable recipe was inspired by the famous dish made with thin slices of raw filet of beef, created by Guiseppe Cipriani at Harry's Bar in Venice. Here I have used thinly sliced vegetables moistened with olive oil and finished with Parmesan cheese shavings. Any fresh crisp vegetables can be used, but choose those which will create an interesting variety of texture, color, and flavor.

1 Trim the radishes and cut into thin circles. Cut the peppers in half, remove the seeds and white membrane, and cut the flesh into short julienne strips. Peel the carrots and cut into very thin diagonal slices. Remove any coarse strings from the celery and cut into thin slices to form semi-circular pieces. Cut the fennel into thin slivers.

2 Divide the vegetables between 4 large plates and arrange in attractive mounds in the center. Drizzle with enough olive oil to lightly moisten the vegetables. Scatter the Parmesan shavings around them and finish with a few grindings of black pepper. Serve with crusty bread.

Serves 4

12 small crisp red radishes
1 green bell pepper
1 red bell pepper
2 small tender young carrots
2–3 celery sticks
1 very small fennel bulb
2–3 tablespoons extra-virgin olive oil
1 ounce Parmesan cheese, cut into thin shavings
pepper

Vegetable Carpaccio is shown on the preceding page

raw vegetable platter

Allow about ½–⅔ cup assorted vegetables per person with a selection of 3–4 dips, salsas, and sauces (pages 208–235)

These raw vegetables and salad leaves are eaten with the fingers and served with dips. Hummus made from ground chickpeas (garbanzo beans) and tahini (sesame seed paste) is good with raw vegetables, so too are guacamole and tapenade, a Provençal olive paste. Pesto, a classic Italian sauce flavored with sweet basil, is also served with raw vegetables, as are numerous uncooked tomato-based sauces and relishes from Mexico called salsas. Raw vegetables are the perfect start to any meal because they are light and refreshing and can be eaten informally with drinks or at the dining table. They also make a healthy lunch or snack with crusty bread as well as excellent party or finger food.

1 Choose firm, crisp vegetables, such as carrots, celery, cucumber, fennel, chicory, peppers, spring onions and lettuce hearts. These can be cut into finger-length pieces or sticks. Tight-headed vegetables, such as broccoli or cauliflower, can be broken into flowerets and small whole vegetables like cherry tomatoes, mushrooms, snowpeas, green beans, and radishes can be left just as they are.

2 Wash and dry the vegetables well, then arrange them on a serving platter or individual plates.

3 Serve the dips, salsas and sauces separately.

vegetable beignets

Serve these crisp, puffy vegetable fritters with either Aïoli (page 223) or Sweet-&-Sour Sauce (page 228.) The key to success, apart from using a varied selection of fresh vegetables, is the batter. After experimenting with many recipes, I believe this Japanese tempura batter is just right.

1 Cut the peppers lengthwise into ⅛–¼ inch strips. Cut the zucchini into flat batons about ¾ x 1½ x ⅛ inch and the eggplant into slices on the diagonal about ⅛ inch thick. Cut the corn in half lengthwise, the onions into rings, and the French beans into 1½ inch lengths. Cut the cauliflower into flowerets and par-boil them for 2 minutes. Drain and refresh. Leave the mushrooms whole if small, or cut in half or in quarters if large.

2 About 20 minutes before cooking, prepare the batter. With a small wire whisk, beat the egg in a large bowl. Still beating, add the lager beer in a thin stream. Sift the flour, baking powder, and a pinch of salt into another bowl, stir in pepper to taste and tip on top of the egg and lager. Stir with the whisk, barely enough to mix. Don't overbeat. Cover and leave to stand for about 10 minutes.

3 Heat the oil in a deep-fryer to 375 degrees. Dip the vegetables in the batter, one type at a time. Fry no more than 6 pieces at once or the temperature of the oil will drop and make the batter greasy. Zucchini, onions, cauliflower, baby corn, and mushrooms take 3–5 minutes; bell peppers, eggplant, and beans about 3 minutes. The batter should be puffy, crisp and golden, the vegetables just tender.

4 Transfer the vegetables to an ovenproof dish or pan lined with parchment paper and keep warm in a preheated oven at 375 degrees. They will hold quite successfully for about 30 minutes.

5 Arrange the beignets on a large platter around a bowl of sauce, or pile about 9 beignets in the center of each individual plate and put a few spoonfuls of sauce on the side. Garnish with herbs or salad leaves and serve immediately.

Serves 6–8

1½ pounds assorted vegetables, such as peppers, zucchini, eggplant, baby corn, onions, green beans, cauliflower, and mushrooms
sunflower oil, for frying
fresh herbs or salad leaves, to garnish

Batter:
1 large egg
1 cup lager beer, very well chilled
½ cup all-purpose flour
½ teaspoon baking powder
salt and pepper

vegetable pakoras

The size of these spicy Indian fritters can vary depending on whether they are to be served as a starter or cocktail snack. Served with cucumber raita, salad, and relishes they are also delicious as an entrée. Any combination of finely sliced or chopped vegetables can be used, as long as the total weight is 12–15 ounces (about 3–4 cups) for the amount of batter given here. Gram flour is available from east Indian stores.

1 Make the batter. Sift the gram flour into a bowl, add the chili powder, salt, baking powder, dry spices, and thyme along with the crushed garlic and ginger. Gradually blend in the water to form a smooth batter of dropping consistency. Stir in the oil.

2 Add the prepared vegetables to the batter and stir to combine.

3 Heat the oil in a deep-fryer to 325–375 degrees. When ready, drop dessert-spoons or teaspoons of the prepared vegetables directly into the hot oil. Keep the wire basket in the pan but don't use it except to lift the pakoras out. Fry about 6 pakoras at a time, depending on their size, for about 4–5 minutes until crisp and golden. Remove from the oil, and drain on paper towels.

4 Garnish the pakoras with lemon wedges and coriander (cilantro) leaves and serve immediately, with cucumber and mint raita.

Makes 25–30 large pakoras to serve 5–6 as a starter, or 50–60 small pakoras to serve 16–20 as a cocktail snack

6 tablespoons minced onion
6 tablespoons potato, peeled and finely diced
1 cup tiny cauliflower sprigs
1 small red bell pepper, cored, seeded, and finely chopped
vegetable oil, for deep-frying

Batter:
1½ cups gram (chickpea) flour
1–2 teaspoons chili powder
1–2 teaspoons salt
1 teaspoon baking powder
3 teaspoons ground cumin
3 teaspoons ground coriander (cilantro)
3 teaspoons pepper
3 teaspoons dried thyme
3 garlic cloves, crushed
½–1 inch piece of fresh root ginger, peeled and grated
1–1¼ cups cold water
2 teaspoons vegetable oil
Cucumber & Mint Raita (page 216), to serve

To Garnish:
lemon wedges
coriander (cilantro) leaves

leek & spinach
phyllo triangles

These are a variation on boerek, *the deep-fried pastries filled with minced meat or cheese from Turkey. They make excellent finger food to serve with pre-dinner or party drinks or, as in this recipe, with fromage frais as a first course. The preparation of phyllo pastry is long and complicated, so ready-made frozen phyllo is generally used. It is widely available from Greek and Middle Eastern food stores and supermarkets. Once defrosted, it quickly dries out and becomes brittle, so work with one sheet at a time, keeping the rest covered with plastic wrap and a damp cloth.*

1 Wash and pick over the fresh spinach and remove any tough central stalks. Shake off the surplus water, leaving only that which clings to the leaves.

2 Heat half of the butter in a large saucepan and fry the onion, garlic, and leek until soft but not colored. Add the spinach and stir to combine. Cover the pan tightly with a lid and cook over a moderate heat for 5–8 minutes until the spinach has wilted and is tender and all the liquid has evaporated. Shake the pan occasionally to prevent it sticking.

3 Squeeze the spinach to remove any excess moisture, leave to cool, then stir in the feta and ricotta, nutmeg, pepper, and beaten egg.

4 Melt the remaining butter and work with 1 sheet of pastry at a time, brushing each one with butter before peeling it off the pile. If you are using the smaller phyllo sheets, fold each one in half lengthwise and place 1 heaped tablespoon of the spinach mixture on one of the short ends. Fold the left corner over the filling and continue folding until you have a pastry triangle with a small flap to tuck underneath. Brush with a little more butter and place on an oiled baking sheet. Repeat to make 14 triangles. If you are using the large sheets of phyllo, put 2 sheets on top of each other then cut into five 3½-inch strips, each 12 inches long. Brush with butter, fill, and roll in the same way to form triangles. Repeat with the remaining pastry to make 15 triangles.

5 Bake in a preheated 375 degree oven for 25–35 minutes, or until golden brown. Garnish with chervil or parsley sprigs and serve warm or at room temperature, with fromage frais or thick plain yogurt.

Makes 14–15 triangles, enough to serve 7

2 cups fresh spinach, or ½ cup
   frozen spinach, defrosted
⅓ cup butter
⅓ cup minced onion
2 garlic cloves, minced
I small leek, thinly sliced
I½ ounces feta cheese, crumbled
I½ ounces ricotta cheese
pinch of freshly grated nutmeg
I small egg, beaten
14 sheets fresh phyllo pastry, each
   12½ x 7 inches, or 6 sheets frozen
   phyllo pastry, each 17½ x 12 inches,
   defrosted
pepper

To Serve:
chervil or flat leaf parsley sprigs
fromage frais or thick natural yogurt

goat's cheese
with peppers & pine nuts

If you don't want to go to the trouble of coating the cheese before baking, you can leave it plain, or simply roll it in toasted bread crumbs. For a speckled coating, add some chopped fresh herbs to the nut and bread crumb mixture.

3 tablespoons pine nuts, toasted
  (below right)

1 tablespoon fresh bread crumbs,
  toasted

½ tablespoon finely chopped basil

1 small garlic clove, minced

2 x 2½ ounce crottins de Chavignol
  goat cheeses, halved

1 tablespoon pine nut or hazelnut oil

4 small roasted red peppers
  (page 83), peeled, seeded, and cut
  into slivers

1 quantity Vinaigrette (page 231)

To Garnish:

12 small basil leaves

8 whole chives

1 Chop 1 tablespoon of the toasted pine nuts and combine them with the bread crumbs, chopped basil, and garlic. Brush each piece of cheese lightly with oil, then coat evenly in the nutty crumbs. Set on a lightly oiled cookie sheet and bake in a preheated 400 degree oven for 8–10 minutes, or until the cheese is warmed through and beginning to melt at the edges.

2 Arrange the pepper slivers on 4 large serving plates. Carefully lift the cheese off the cookie sheet and set on top of the peppers. Shake the dressing and drizzle a little over each serving. Garnish with the reserved whole toasted pine nuts, the basil leaves and chives and serve immediately.

Serves 4

TOASTED PINE NUTS Spread the pine nuts on a heavy baking sheet and toast under a preheated hot broiler, tossing frequently until an even golden color. Don't overbrown the nuts or they will taste bitter.

broiled asparagus

Cooked on a ridged cast iron grill pan or over a barbecue, asparagus has an entirely different taste and texture from boiled or steamed asparagus, particularly if it has been allowed to singe and brown a little, which gives it a rich flavor. Choose fine asparagus spears about ½ inch in diameter.

1 Melt the butter with the oil in a small saucepan over a low heat. Lay the prepared spears on a preheated very hot broiler pan or barbecue, and brush with the oil and butter mixture. Reduce the heat slightly to allow the asparagus to cook through without burning, and cook for about 5 minutes without moving. Turn the asparagus, brush again with the oil and butter, and cook for a further 5 minutes until the asparagus is tender, well seared and slightly wilted.

2 Remove the asparagus from the broiler or grill with tongs, and serve on a warmed plate. Season with the rock salt and black pepper, and garnish with the lemon. A little fine quality olive oil or melted butter can also be drizzled over the asparagus if desired, and few fresh Parmesan cheese shavings also make an excellent addition.

Serves 1

2 tablespoons butter
1–2 tablespoons light olive oil
6–8 fresh asparagus spears, trimmed
rock salt and black pepper
¼ lemon, to garnish

Grilled Asparagus is shown on page 256

mushroom
& green herb pâté

This succulent, earthy pâté can be made with one type of mushroom, such as the white button mushrooms available everywhere, or the large open-cap variety which have a more definite flavor. If expense is no object, a few fresh or dried wild mushrooms will give the pâté a more intense, fuller flavor. Serve with fingers of toast, warm pita bread, crostini, or savory crackers. For a more elegant presentation, mold the pâté into four individual ramekin dishes lined with plastic wrap, leave to set, then unmold to serve. Sliced sautéed mushrooms can be sandwiched between a bottom and top layer of pâté in the ramekins, or mushrooms piled on top when the pâté is unmolded.

2 tablespoons light olive oil

4 tablespoons unsalted butter

1 small onion, finely chopped

1–2 garlic cloves, crushed

2 cups mushrooms, sliced

1 teaspoon ground coriander

1 teaspoon mushroom ketchup (optional)

dash of Worcestershire sauce

½ cup low-fat cream cheese

1 tablespoon fine brown bread crumbs

2 tablespoons finely chopped coriander (cilantro)

2 tablespoons minced flat leaf parsley

2 tablespoons clarified butter (below right)

salt and pepper

1 Heat the oil and butter in a large skillet and fry the onion and garlic over a gentle heat until soft but not colored. Increase the heat and add the mushrooms. Fry until all the moisture has been driven off and the mushrooms are a rich toasty golden brown color. This will take about 15 minutes.

2 Add the ground coriander and fry for a few minutes to develop the flavor. Add the mushroom ketchup (if using) and the Worcestershire sauce, stirring to remove any sediment from the base of the pan. Allow to cool slightly, then turn into a food processor or blender. Add the cream cheese, bread crumbs, coriander (cilantro), and parsley and process until well blended, stopping and starting the machine several times to scrape the mixture well down on to the blades. The pâté can be processed until very smooth or left with a little texture, depending on taste. Season with salt and pepper.

3 Pile the pâté into either 1 large or 4 individual bowls, level the surface and pour a little clarified butter on top. Cover with plastic wrap and refrigerate until required. Allow the pâté to return to room temperature about 1 hour before serving, otherwise the flavors will be masked by the cold.

Serves 4

TO CLARIFY BUTTER Melt the butter in a saucepan over a low heat. Using a spoon, skim off the froth from the surface and discard. Set a sieve lined with cheesecloth over a bowl and carefully pour through the clear, melted butter and leave to settle. Gently pour into another bowl, leaving the milky sediment behind. The clarified butter is now ready for use.

rustic Greek salad

There are a few classic combinations of ingredients that are so perfect they require no embellishment. This peasant salad, known as horiatiki *in Greek, is one of them. To capture it at its best, use only the finest quality ingredients.*

1 pound –1 pound 10 ounces
  tomatoes (large, cherry, or
  miniature plum)

7–8 ounces feta cheese, drained and
  cut into ½-inch cubes

1 small red onion, peeled

16 black Greek olives, pitted if
  preferred

25 flat leaf parsley leaves

2 tablespoons lemon juice

4–5 tablespoons light extra virgin
  olive oil

salt and pepper

warm pita bread, to serve

1 If using large tomatoes, cut them in half lengthwise, then cut each half into 3 wedges. If using baby tomatoes, cut them in half lengthwise. Put into a large bowl with the feta.

2 Cut the onion into quarters, then cut each quarter into 4 sections. Scatter with the tomatoes and cheese. Add the olives and parsley leaves.

3 Pour over the lemon juice and toss very gently to coat. Use 2 wooden spoons or your fingers so as not to break the tomato flesh or the cheese. Pour over the oil and toss again, seasoning with salt and pepper. Serve the salad immediately, with warm pita bread.

Serves 8

eggs Florentine

A divine combination of lightly cooked egg and meltingly tender spinach finished with a topping of crème fraîche, Cheddar, and Parmesan cheeses. Perfect as a first course, light lunch or snack. Frozen spinach can be used if fresh is not available, in which case allow 1 pound.

1 Wash and pick over the spinach, discarding any tough central stalks and damaged or discolored leaves. Rinse and drain, leaving only the water that clings to the leaves.

2 Melt half of the butter in a large saucepan, add the spinach, cover tightly, and sweat until the leaves have wilted, the spinach is tender, and any liquid has evaporated. Transfer to a large sieve or colander and squeeze out any liquid that remains. Return to the pan and season with nutmeg, salt and pepper.

3 Brush six individual gratin dishes with the remaining butter. Divide the spinach between them, making a well in the center for an egg and leaving a ½ inch space at the top.

4 Mix the crème fraîche and cream. Break an egg into the center of each gratin dish and dust with salt and pepper. Spoon the cream mixture evenly over the eggs and sprinkle with the Cheddar and Parmesan.

5 Set the gratin dishes on a heavy cookie sheet and bake in a preheated 425-degree oven for about 10–12 minutes until the whites are set but the yolks are still runny.

6 Remove the dishes from the oven and place under a preheated hot broiler until the topping is bubbling and the cheese golden brown. Serve immediately.

Serves 6

8 cups fresh spinach
3 tablespoons butter
a little freshly grated nutmeg
salt and pepper
6 large eggs

Topping:
⅔ cup crème fraîche
¼ cup heavy cream
3 tablespoons grated Cheddar cheese
3 tablespoons Parmesan cheese,
  freshly grated
salt and pepper

spinach & ricotta gnocchi

These bright green savory dumplings from Tuscany are usually eaten as an appetizer. They are also excellent as an entrée, served simply with lots of melted butter and Parmesan cheese as in this recipe, or dressed with a thin, creamy béchamel or tomato sauce and a dusting of cheese, then broiled until bubbling and golden.

1 Wash and pick over the spinach, discarding any tough central stalks and damaged or discolored leaves. Rinse and drain, leaving only the water that clings to the leaves. Cover and cook for a few minutes until the leaves are wilted and tender. Increase the heat to drive off any remaining water. Squeeze dry and leave to cool.

2 Put the spinach, ricotta, egg yolks, Parmesan, nutmeg, sage leaves, and salt and pepper into a food processor and work to a smooth purée. Turn into a bowl, sift the flour over the mixture, and mix to form a dough. Cover with plastic wrap and leave in the refrigerator for about 15 minutes.

3 Meanwhile, prepare the dressing. Melt the butter and gently fry the chili in it until soft. Keep warm.

4 Using well-floured hands, take a tablespoon at a time of the gnocchi mixture and shape into small ovals or egg shapes. As each gnocchi is made, place it on a lightly floured cookie sheet until ready to cook.

5 Bring about 3½ quarts salted water to a boil in a large wide pan, reduce the heat to a simmer, and poach 6 gnocchi at a time for 4–5 minutes, or until they are puffy and have risen to the surface. Remove with a slotted spoon and pile into warmed individual dishes.

6 Pour the chili butter over them, sprinkle with the Parmesan cheese and shredded sage leaves, and serve immediately.

Makes 24, to serve 8 as a starter or 4 as an entrée

6 cups fresh spinach
¾ –1 cup ricotta cheese
2 egg yolks
4 tablespoons Parmesan cheese, freshly grated
¼ teaspoon freshly grated nutmeg
2 sage leaves, finely chopped
4 tablespoons all-purpose flour
a little extra flour, for shaping
salt and pepper

To Serve:
6 tablespoons butter
1 small red chili pepper, seeded and finely chopped
1 cup freshly grated Parmesan cheese
6–8 sage leaves, shredded

potato gnocchi
with pesto sauce

Gnocchi are light, airy little dumplings from the north of Italy. In Genoa, where this recipe comes from, they are served with pesto. The secret of making successful gnocchi is in the quality and dryness of the potatoes (Burbank Russets are suitable), the proportion of flour to potato, light mixing and handling, and careful cooking.

1 Bake the potatoes in a preheated 400 degree oven, for about 1 hour until tender. Leave to cool slightly.

2 Peel the cooled potatoes and measure the cooked flesh, you should have about 3 cups. Mash or press through a potato ricer while still hot. Season well with salt, pepper, and nutmeg. Sift on the flour, add the beaten egg and use a wooden spoon to bring it together as lightly as possible and form a soft dough. Do not overwork or the gnocchi will be tough and heavy.

3 Divide the dough into quarters. Lightly dust your hands and work surface with a little flour and roll each into a sausage ¾ inch in diameter, then cut into ½-inch pieces. Dust lightly with flour and put the gnocchi pieces on a floured board. Cover with plastic wrap and chill for 30 minutes.

4 Press each gnocchi on to the prongs of a fork, to make a ridged pattern, then set on a floured board ready for poaching. The ridges provide grooves to hold the butter or sauce which will coat them.

5 Brush a shallow baking dish with the melted butter. Fill a large saucepan three-quarters full of unsalted water and bring to a boil. Add one-third of the gnocchi and simmer gently until they float to the surface (this will take about 3 minutes), then cook for a further 20–30 seconds.

6 Lift the gnocchi out of the water with a slotted spoon, drain, and put into the buttered dish. Keep warm while cooking the remaining gnocchi in batches. Pour a little of the remaining butter over the gnocchi between each batch.

7 Make the sauce. Melt the butter in a pan, stir in the pesto, and heat gently until it bubbles. Divide the gnocchi between warmed plates and coat with the pesto. Garnish with the basil and serve, with grated Parmesan.

Serves 8

2 pounds floury baking potatoes
1–2 teaspoons salt
pepper
pinch of freshly grated nutmeg
2 cups self-rising flour
1 medium egg, beaten
a little extra flour, for rolling
1 tablespoon butter, melted

Sauce:
4 tablespoons butter
⅔ cup Pesto (page 234)

To Serve:
fresh basil sprigs
2 tablespoons Parmesan cheese,
 freshly grated

asparagus
& white wine risotto

Risotto with asparagus is one of my favorite dishes, and perfect for a light first or main course lunch or supper in spring. It is easy to make, and you will achieve perfect results if you follow my method — and use the correct rice of course.

1½ quarts light vegetable broth or
  water
1 pound young green asparagus
  (whole stems), trimmed and peeled,
  with trimmings reserved
1 bay leaf
2 large onions, 1 quartered and
  1 minced
½ cup unsalted butter
1½–2 cups short-grain rice
1¼ cups dry white wine
4 tablespoons Parmesan cheese,
  thinly shaved
salt and pepper

1 Bring the broth or water to a boil, put in the asparagus trimmings, the bay leaf, and onion quarters and boil for 20 minutes. Strain into another pan and return the broth to a boil.

2 Meanwhile, cut the asparagus tips into 1–1½ inch lengths. Cut half of the remaining stems into similar-sized pieces and chop the rest very finely. Cook the asparagus tips and pieces of stem in the boiling broth for 3–4 minutes depending on their thickness, until just tender. Transfer the asparagus to a colander with a slotted spoon and refresh under cold running water until completely cold. Drain and reserve. Keep the stock simmering.

3 Melt half of the butter in a large heavy pan over a low heat. Add the chopped onion and cook gently until soft and transparent but not colored. It is important to cook it gently or the butter will burn and brown. Stir in the dry unwashed rice and cook, stirring constantly, until the rice becomes opaque. Add the wine and boil for 1 minute, stirring all the time.

4 Add a ladleful of simmering broth and stir until it is absorbed, then add another ladleful and repeat the process until nearly all the broth has been absorbed and the rice is almost cooked. This will take about 15 minutes. Stir constantly to prevent the rice sticking and ensure even cooking.

5 Add the asparagus with the remaining broth and continue cooking, stirring carefully, until the asparagus is tender and the rice creamy. Stir in the remaining butter and season with salt and pepper. Serve immediately in soup plates, topped with Parmesan shavings.

Serves 4

CHEF'S TIP Leftover risotto can be mixed with a little beaten egg and the mixture dropped in tablespoonfuls into hot butter in a skillet, and pressed into little cakes. Cook for a few minutes until golden brown on each side.

stews

spicy beef koftas
in pizzaiola sauce

Serve as an entrée with noodles or rice and a crisp mixed leaf salad. Or make miniature koftas and serve as a cocktail savory on sticks, with the sauce considerably reduced and served as a dip. The sauce is also good with pasta and gnocchi. Chicken or lamb can be used for the meatballs instead of the beef.

1 First make the koftas. Beat the egg in a large bowl, stir in the bread crumbs, and add the beef and onion. Season with salt and pepper. Work together until well combined. You will find that your hands are best for this. Divide the mixture into 8 portions, shape each one into a ball, and roll in a little flour. Heat the oil in a large skillet and fry the koftas until evenly browned, turning frequently. This will take about 10 minutes.

2 Meanwhile, prepare the sauce. Heat the oil in a saucepan and fry the onion and garlic until soft but not colored. Add the remaining ingredients, except half of the olives. Bring to the boil and cook over a high heat for 10 minutes to concentrate the flavors and slightly reduce the liquid.

3 Using a slotted spoon, lower the koftas into the sauce. Cover and cook gently for about 30 minutes until the meat is cooked through and the sauce rich and pulpy. Remove about 4 tablespoons of the sauce and a few olives and process to a thick purée in a food processor or blender. Stir into the sauce. Taste and adjust the seasoning, if necessary, and garnish with the parsley sprigs and remaining olives before serving.

Serves 4

Koftas:
1 medium egg
4 tablespoons coarse bread crumbs
1 pound lean ground beef
6 tablespoons grated onion
2 tablespoons all-purpose flour
2 tablespoons sunflower or olive oil
salt and pepper

Pizzaiola Sauce:
1–2 tablespoons sunflower or olive oil
1 large onion, finely chopped
2 garlic cloves, crushed
1 red chili pepper, seeded and finely chopped
1–2 red peppers, cored, seeded and chopped
1 x 13 ounce can plum tomatoes
1¼ cups beef broth
2 tablespoons double concentrate tomato paste
2 tablespoons minced basil
1 teaspoon minced oregano
pinch of sugar
1 tablespoon minced flat leaf parsley
¼–½ cup black Kalamata olives, pitted
flat leaf parsley sprigs, to garnish

Spicy Beef Koftas are shown on the preceding page

Breton beans
with cheese & herb crust

Any combination of fresh vegetables and beans can be used to make this dish, and it makes an excellent entrée served with a mixed leaf salad. Alternatively, prepare the vegetable stew without the cheese & herb crust and serve it as an accompaniment to roast or braised leg of lamb.

3 tablespoons olive oil

2 large onions, finely sliced

2–3 garlic cloves, chopped

2 large zucchini, about 1 pound, cut into ½ inch dice

2 red peppers, cored, seeded, and diced

2 x 13-ounce cans chopped plum tomatoes

1 tablespoon double concentrate tomato paste

2 x 13-ounce cans lima or navy beans, drained

⅔ cup vegetable broth

1 tablespoon minced basil

1 bay leaf

1 teaspoon sugar

salt and pepper

Cheese & Herb Crust:

1 small French loaf, very thinly sliced

2 tablespoons olive oil

2 tablespoons minced basil

1 tablespoon minced parsley

4 tablespoons finely grated Parmesan cheese

1 Heat the oil in a large saucepan or flameproof casserole and fry the onions and garlic until soft but not colored. Add the zucchini and continue to fry for a few minutes until beginning to color. Add all the remaining ingredients, except salt, and stir well to combine. Bring the mixture to a boil, reduce the heat, cover, and simmer until the tomatoes are thick and pulpy and the flavors blended. This will take about 30–40 minutes. Taste and adjust the seasoning, adding salt if necessary.

2 Uncover the stew. Brush the bread slices with oil, arrange on top of the stew and scatter with the herbs and Parmesan. Toast under a preheated broiler until the bread is golden-brown and crisp. Serve immediately.

Serves 6

saffron-spiced
vegetable couscous

Couscous combines delicate velvety grains and fragrant spicy stew. It is traditionally made of meat, generally lamb or chicken, with several different types of vegetables. In this recipe I have concentrated solely on the vegetables. Couscous is a wonderful combination of tastes, textures, colors, and smells, and, although the list of ingredients may look daunting, the dish itself is as simple to prepare as any stew.

1 Put the couscous into a large bowl and cover with the water. Leave to soak for 10 minutes, then fork through and leave for a further 10 minutes.

2 Meanwhile, prepare the sauce. Heat half of the oil in a large saucepan. Fry the onions until beginning to brown, then add the garlic and ginger. Stir in the ground spices and cinnamon stick and fry for a few minutes. Add the soaked saffron to the pan with the broth, tomatoes, tomato paste, and chili sauce. Bring to a boil.

3 Add the carrots and turnips to the sauce, reduce the heat, cover, and cook for about 10 minutes. Meanwhile, heat the rest of the oil in a large skillet and fry the fennel wedges until lightly colored. Transfer to the sauce with a slotted spoon. Fry the eggplant and zucchini until browning, adding a little extra oil if necessary. Drain and add to the sauce. Cook gently for 15–20 minutes until the vegetables are tender and the sauce rich and thick. During this final cooking, steam the couscous.

4 To serve, pile the couscous in a large dish, fleck with pieces of butter, and stir in with a fork. Stir the chopped coriander (cilantro) into the stew. Serve a mound of couscous to each person, spoon the vegetable stew on top, and garnish with coriander (cilantro) sprigs.

Serves 6

1¾–2 cups pre-cooked couscous

1¼ cups water

8 ounces carrots, cut into
   ¾ inch chunks

2 small turnips, cut into
   ¾ inch chunks

1–2 large fennel bulbs, each cut into
   6 wedges

1 large eggplant, cut into
   ¾ inch cubes

4 zucchini, cut into ¾ inch slices

4 tablespoons butter

2–3 tablespoons finely chopped
   coriander (cilantro)

salt

coriander (cilantro) sprigs, to garnish

Sweet Spicy Sauce:

8 tablespoons extra virgin olive oil

2 large onions, cut into wedges

4 garlic cloves, crushed

1 inch piece of fresh root
   ginger, peeled and grated

1 tablespoon each ground cumin and
   coriander

1 teaspoon each turmeric, paprika
   and black pepper

2-inch piece cinnamon stick

1 teaspoon saffron threads, soaked in
   2 tablespoons warm water

3 cups vegetable broth

2 x 13-ounce cans chopped
   tomatoes

2 tablespoons tomato paste

2 tablespoons sweet chili sauce

Mexican bean stew
with avocado & tomato salsa

A fiery stew of mixed vegetables and beans, an updated version of the classic chili con carne without the meat. Vegetables such as onions, red and green peppers, carrot and celery give an excellent texture and variety of color. They are then spiked with garlic and chili peppers, enriched with two varieties of kidney bean — red and black — and cooked in a sauce of tomato, coriander (cilantro), and lime until rich and thick. Serve with tortilla chips and/or basmati rice for an entrée or party dish.

1 Heat the oil in a large saucepan and fry the onions, garlic, and chili peppers for about 10 minutes until soft but not colored. Add the vegetables, half of the coriander, the lime juice, tomato paste, tomatoes, and vegetable broth. Stir well to combine, bring to a boil, and cook for 30 minutes.

2 Add the beans, cover, and simmer for 15 minutes until the vegetables are tender and the sauce thick and pulpy. Ten minutes before the end of cooking, add the diced peppers.

3 Remove 2 soup ladlefuls of the cooked stew and blend in a food processor. This will give extra body and substance to the stew. Return to the pan, stirring to combine. Add the sugar, season with salt and pepper, and add the remaining chopped coriander (cilantro.)

Serve immediately in large soup plates, each portion topped with 1 tablespoon fromage frais, a little of the salsa, and a sprig of fresh coriander (cilantro.)

Serves 6–8

2–3 tablespoons sunflower oil

2 large onions, minced

2 garlic cloves, crushed

2 green chili peppers, seeded and chopped

1 pound mixed vegetables, such as 2 celery sticks, 2 medium carrots, 1 large zucchini, 1 medium parsnip, all cut into ½ inch cubes

3 tablespoons finely chopped coriander (cilantro)

1 tablespoon lime juice

2 tablespoons double concentrate tomato paste

2 x 13 ounce cans chopped tomatoes

2 cups vegetable broth

1 x 13 ounce can red kidney beans, drained

1 x 13 ounce can black kidney beans, drained

2 large red bell peppers, cored, seeded and diced

a pinch of sugar

salt and pepper

To Serve:

6–8 tablespoons fromage frais

Avocado & Tomato Salsa (page 212)

6–8 coriander (cilantro) sprigs

spinach & chickpea stew

The combination of fresh tangy green spinach and the rich nutty flavor of pale golden chickpeas (garbanzo beans) give this rustic stew a most delicious flavor. It is a very useful standby dish because it can be quickly made from pantry ingredients. Serve with thick plain yogurt and a mixed leaf salad.

1 Blend half of the chickpeas (garbanzo beans) in a food processor or blender, adding enough broth to give a smooth paste.

2 Wash and pick over the spinach, discarding any tough central stalks damaged or discolored leaves. Rinse and drain, then put the spinach into a large saucepan with only the water that clings to the leaves. Cover tightly with a piece of foil and a lid and cook gently until tender, turning and shaking occasionally. This will take about 4 minutes.

3 Heat the oil in a large saucepan and fry the onions and garlic until soft but not colored. Add the cumin and paprika along with the whole chickpeas (garbanzo beans) and fry for a few minutes, stirring well. Add the spinach, tomatoes, tomato paste, chickpea purée, and oregano. Season with salt and pepper. Bring to a boil, reduce the heat and simmer for 5–10 minutes until the flavors are blended and the stew rich and pulpy.

4 Stir in half of the Cheddar cheese until just melted, then divide between four to six individual gratin dishes. Mix the remaining Cheddar and Parmesan cheeses together and sprinkle over the stew. Broil under a hot broiler until the cheese is bubbling and forms a golden crust. Serve immediately.

Serves 4–6

2 x 13 ounce cans chickpeas
  (garbanzo beans), drained
½–⅔ cup vegetable broth
4 cups fresh spinach
2–3 tablespoons olive oil
1–2 large onions, finely chopped
2–4 garlic cloves, crushed
2 teaspoons ground cumin
2 teaspoons paprika
2 x 13 ounce cans plum tomatoes
1 tablespoon double concentrate
  tomato paste
2 teaspoons finely chopped oregano
4 tablespoons grated mature farm-
  house Cheddar cheese
2 tablespoons freshly grated
  Parmesan cheese,
salt and pepper

green vegetables
with Thai-spiced coconut sauce

Any combination of crunchy seasonal green vegetables can be used, as long as they offer variety in shape and texture. For a non-vegetarian alternative, finger strips of raw chicken breast can be added to the sauce with the vegetables. Serve with boiled rice.

¾ cup snowpeas, topped and tailed
  and halved on the diagonal, if large
2 large zucchini, cut into ¼ inch slices
½ cup shelled peas
1 cup broccoli flowerets, trimmed
½ red chili, seeded and sliced,
  to garnish

Coconut Sauce:
3 tablespoons vegetable oil
1 large onion, finely chopped
4 garlic cloves, finely chopped
3–4 teaspoons green Thai curry paste
2 teaspoons turmeric
2 teaspoons brown sugar
2 x 13-ounce cans coconut milk
juice of ½ lime
3 tablespoons dried shredded
  unsweetened coconut
¾ cup vegetable broth
1 tablespoon cornstarch
4 tablespoons heavy cream
4 tablespoons minced coriander
  (cilantro)
salt and pepper

1 First make the sauce. Heat the oil in a large saucepan and fry the onion and garlic until soft but not colored. Stir in the curry paste, turmeric, sugar, coconut milk, lime juice, shredded coconut, and broth, mixing well to blend. Bring to a boil and cook quickly, stirring frequently, for 10–15 minutes to reduce the sauce slightly and concentrate the flavors.

2 Blend the cornstarch with the cream to make a smooth paste, add to the sauce and cook for a few minutes to thicken, then stir in half of the coriander. Add the snowpeas, zucchini, and peas and simmer gently.

3 Steam the broccoli for 4 minutes, then add to the sauce and cook for a few minutes until all the vegetables are tender. Season to taste, sprinkle with the remaining coriander (cilantro), garnish with chili slices, and serve immediately.

Serves 4

fragrant mixed vegetable stew

This rich vegetable stew in tones of orange, green, and gold was inspired by the exotic blend of spices used in Indian cooking, more often fragrant than hot and fiery. The vegetables chosen have a variety of taste, color, and texture, but any balanced selection could be used. I suggest limiting the number to six plus the onion so that the stew does not become a confusion of flavors and tastes. Serve with white or brown basmati rice, natural yogurt or Cucumber & Mint Raita (page 216) and Mung Dhal (page 251.)

1 Heat the oil in a large saucepan and fry the onions and garlic until golden. Stir in the curry paste and fry, stirring for a few minutes to develop the flavors. Stir in the tomato paste. Mix the coconut cream with the boiling water and add to the pan with the lime juice and sugar. Bring to a boil and cook for about 20 minutes to reduce and concentrate the flavors.

2 Add the carrot, new potatoes, and sweet potato and stir well. Bring to a boil, then reduce the heat and simmer for 25 minutes until the vegetables are almost tender.

3 Add the beans and cauliflower (if using), cover, and cook over a low heat for 10–20 minutes until the vegetables are almost tender. Add the broccoli (if using) and cook for 4–5 minutes. Taste, season with salt as necessary and stir in the chopped coriander. Serve immediately, garnished with coriander sprigs.

Serves 6

4 tablespoons vegetable oil

2 large onions, minced

6 garlic cloves, minced

4 tablespoons mild curry paste

½ teaspoon double concentrate tomato paste

2 cups coconut cream

2 cups boiling water

2 tablespoons lime juice

1 tablespoon brown sugar

8 ounces carrot, cut into 1 x ¾ inch chunks

1 cup small new potatoes, halved lengthwise

8 ounces sweet potato, cut into ½ inch cubes

1 cup green beans, trimmed and halved

1 cup cauliflower or broccoli flowerets

2 tablespoons finely chopped coriander (cilantro)

salt

coriander sprigs, to garnish

fricassée of mushrooms

This simple stew of wild and cultivated mushrooms in its rich garlic and herb sauce is one of the countryside's great gifts to the enthusiastic cook. Any edible mushrooms can be used, but my favorite combination is chanterelles, ceps, trompettes des morts, puffballs, and a few field or button mushrooms. It is a quick and easy dish to prepare and has many different uses. In late summer and early fall I've served it perched on a croûte of fried potato bread and topped with a fried egg. I've also enjoyed it as a light lunch or supper dish piled on crostini, bruschetta, or fingers of toast. For a cocktail savory, I chop the mushrooms more finely, pile them into miniature pastry cases, and serve them hot or cold with drinks. In this recipe, I suggest serving the fricassée with broiled polenta cakes for a substantial main course. For a first course to serve six, allow 2 polenta triangles per person.

½ cup unsalted butter

1 large onion, minced

2 garlic cloves, minced

2 pounds mixed mushrooms, brushed, cleaned and sliced if large

2 tablespoons minced parsley

¾ cup red wine

1 egg yolk

1 teaspoon arrowroot

4 tablespoons heavy cream

2 tablespoons finely snipped chives

salt and pepper

small bunch of arugula, to garnish

Polenta Cakes (page 250), to serve

1 Melt the butter in a very large skillet and fry the onion and garlic until soft but not colored. Add the mushrooms and cover with a lid or sheet of aluminum foil. Cook over a gentle heat for about 10 minutes to draw out their juices — at this stage the mushrooms should stew rather than fry.

2 Add the parsley and red wine to the mushrooms. Bring to a boil, then cook gently over a low heat for a few minutes. Blend the egg yolk with the arrowroot and cream and use to thicken the wine and mushroom juices. Stir in the chives and season with salt and pepper.

3 Arrange the mushroom fricassée on warm plates with 3 polenta triangles to accompany each serving. Garnish with arugula leaves and serve immediately.

Serves 4

hot spiced stew with
potatoes & cauliflower

Stews made with vegetables can be light and subtle or richly spiced and substantial. The possibilities are endless. In this simple but flavorsome stew, potatoes, cauliflower, lentils, and spices are combined to produce a colorful and tasty entrée.

1 Rinse the lentils or split peas under cold running water, drain, and put into a large saucepan with half of the broth. Bring to a boil, then reduce the heat, and simmer for 30 minutes until the lentils or split peas are soft and all the liquid has been absorbed.

2 While the lentils or split peas are cooking, prepare and cook the vegetables. Heat the oil in a large saucepan, add the onions, and fry over a low heat for about 8 minutes, stirring frequently. Add the potatoes and cauliflower to the pan with the garlic and cook for 1 minute. Stir in the turmeric, mustard, and fennel seeds and the chopped chili peppers, turning and tossing them in the pan. Add the remaining broth and the soaked saffron and bring to a boil. Reduce the heat and cook gently for 10–15 minutes until the vegetables are almost cooked.

3 When the lentils or split peas are cooked, mash them with a potato masher to form a thick purée, leaving a few whole through the mixture. Add the coconut cream and stir well to mix. Add this thick purée to the vegetables and stir well to combine. This will make the stew rich and thick. Season with salt and pepper and cook gently until the vegetables are completely tender and the flavors combined. Stir in the coriander and serve immediately.

Serves 6

1½ cups whole lentils or split yellow peas, rinsed and soaked in water to cover for 15 minutes

1¾ cups vegetable broth

3 tablespoons vegetable oil

2 large onions, cut into wedges

2–2½ pounds potatoes, cut into chunks

1 cauliflower, cut into flowerets and stalks removed

3–4 garlic cloves, crushed

2 teaspoons turmeric

2 tablespoons black mustard seeds

1–2 tablespoons fennel seeds

1–2 small fresh green chili peppers, seeded and chopped

1 teaspoon saffron threads, soaked in 2 tablespoons warm water

½ cup coconut cream

2 tablespoons chopped coriander (cilantro)

salt and pepper

Mediterranean lamb stew
with tomatoes, olives, & pasta

In this recipe I have used leg of lamb because of its sweet taste and the fact that it isn't too fatty. The cubed lamb is simmered in a rich broth of onions, garlic, tomatoes, and herbs until all the flavors have blended and the meat is meltingly tender. Luscious black olives and freshly cooked pasta are stirred in before serving to create a perfect one-dish meal. Serve with salad and garlic bread or pieces of broiled polenta (page 250.)

1 Put the lamb into a non-metallic bowl and cover with the wine. Leave to marinate at room temperature for about 1 hour.

2 Heat 2 tablespoons of the oil in a large skillet and fry the onions and garlic in batches until beginning to brown. Transfer to a casserole and add the chopped chili.

3 Remove the meat from the marinade, reserving the marinade, and drain on paper towels. Fry in the remaining hot oil until browned all over, in batches if necessary. Transfer to the casserole using a slotted spoon.

4 Add the tomatoes, tomato paste, lamb broth, and wine marinade. Tuck the bouquet garni down the side, stir in the olives, and bring the mixture to a boil. Reduce the heat, cover closely with aluminum foil and a lid and simmer very gently on top of the stove or in a preheated 300 degree oven for ¾–1 hour until the meat is almost tender. Keep checking after 30 minutes; overcooked meat will be tough and stringy.

5 While the lamb is cooking, make a paste to thicken the stew by kneading the butter and flour together. Cook the pasta in a large pan of boiling salted water for 7 minutes or according to the package instructions. Drain and refresh in cold water until completely cold.

6 When the stew is cooked, remove the bouquet garni, season well with salt and pepper, and thicken with the beurre manié. Do this by stirring little pieces into the hot stew until you feel it is the correct consistency. Add the pasta and cook for a few minutes to heat through. Serve in warmed large soup plates, sprinkled with the herbs and Parmesan.

Serves 6

2 pounds leg of lamb, trimmed and
   cut into 1½ inch pieces
1¾ cups dry white wine
4–6 tablespoons extra-virgin olive oil
2 large onions, sliced
2 garlic cloves, chopped
1 red chili pepper, seeded and
   chopped
2 x 13 ounce cans chopped
   tomatoes
2 tablespoons double concentrate
   tomato paste
⅔ cup rich lamb broth
1 bouquet garni (2 bay leaves tied
   together with 2 parsley stalks,
   1 sprig each thyme and rosemary,
   and 1 piece of celery stick)
¼ cup black olives
2–3 tablespoons softened butter
2–3 tablespoons all-purpose flour
6 ounces dried cavatellucci,
   garganelli, romagnoli, or other small
   pasta shapes
salt and pepper

To Garnish:
2 tablespoons minced flat leaf parsley
2 tablespoons minced mint
4 tablespoons freshly grated
   Parmesan cheese

vegetable stew
with mustard & herb dumplings

A spicy and versatile stew finished with light-as-air dumplings. Any seasonal vegetables can be used in any combination — in addition to the ones I have used here, turnips and zucchini are particularly delicious. A perfect dish for a fall day.

2 tablespoons olive or sunflower oil

I large onion, sliced

**2 large carrots, cut into
   I inch chunks**

**3–4 celery sticks, cut into
   I inch chunks**

**2 small turnips, cut into
   I inch chunks**

**I pound potatoes, cut into
   I inch chunks**

I x 13 ounce can plum tomatoes

3 cups vegetable broth

2 tablespoon tomato paste

I tablespoon paprika

4 tablespoons chopped parsley

salt and pepper

Dumplings:

I cup self-rising flour

4 tablespoons butter

2 tablespoons minced parsley

**I teaspoon chopped thyme or
   marjoram**

I tablespoon powdered hot mustard

I small egg, beaten

1 Heat the oil in a large saucepan and fry the onion until soft but not colored. Add the carrots, celery, turnip, and potatoes and stir well to combine. Cover closely with aluminum foil and cook very gently over a low heat for about 5 minutes to draw out the flavor of the vegetables.

2 Add the tomatoes, broth, tomato paste, paprika, and half of the parsley, and season with salt and pepper. Bring to a boil, then reduce the heat, cover and simmer gently for 15–20 minutes.

3 Meanwhile, prepare the dumplings. Put the flour into a large bowl, cut the butter into small pieces and rub into the flour using your fingertips until the mixture resembles fine bread crumbs. Stir in the herbs, mustard and season with salt and pepper. Make a well in the center, add the beaten egg, and enough water to form a sticky dough.

4 Using a wet spoon, drop 8 tablespoons of the dough on to the simmering stew. Cover and cook for 20–30 minutes until the vegetables are tender and the dumplings light and fluffy. Sprinkle the remaining parsley over the stew and serve immediately.

Serves 4

caponata

This sweet-and-sour vegetable stew comes from Sicily. Serve it at room temperature with plenty of good country bread and a selection of cold meats, such as salami and ham, or fish. It is also good as a relish with broiled and grilled meats, and makes a tasty topping for bruschetta and crostini.

1¼ cups sunflower oil

3 large eggplant, cut into
  ¾ inch cubes

6 celery sticks, thinly sliced

2–3 tablespoons minced flat leaf
  parsley

Tomato Sauce:

2 tablespoons extra virgin olive oil

1 large onion, minced

1 x 13 ounce can chopped plum
  tomatoes

½ cup red wine vinegar

2 tablespoons brown sugar

4 tablespoons pitted green olives

3 tablespoons salted or pickled
  capers, drained and rinsed

salt and pepper

1 First make the sauce. Heat the oil in a large saucepan and fry the onion over a gentle heat until soft and rich golden-brown. Add the tomatoes and vinegar and boil rapidly for a few minutes to drive off the excess liquid. Stir in the sugar, olives, and capers, then simmer gently for about 20 minutes to form a thick, pulpy mixture.

2 Meanwhile, heat half the sunflower oil in a large skillet and fry the eggplant in batches over a high heat until golden-brown on all sides, adding more oil when necessary. Remove with a slotted spoon and drain on paper towels. Fry the celery in the remaining oil until golden-brown and drain on paper towels.

3 Season the sauce with salt and pepper, adding extra sugar if necessary to give a distinctive sweet-and-sour taste, then add the eggplant and celery, and cook gently for 5–10 minutes. Transfer to a bowl, leave to cool, cover, and refrigerate until required.

4 To serve, bring the caponata to room temperature and sprinkle with chopped parsley. If you plan to store the caponata for several days, float a thin film of olive oil over the top and cover the bowl with plastic wrap or a lid.

Serves 6–8

ratatouille

This is my version of the pungent vegetable stew of Provence, one of the great dishes of the Mediterranean. In the recipe I have roasted the vegetables in the oven before combining them with a stew of tomatoes and herbs. This ensures they keep their texture while at the same time creating a mixture which is rich and thick. Ratatouille can be served hot or cold with crusty bread; as an accompaniment to broiled or roasted meats; as a light first course or snack with eggs; in omelets and as part of a scrambled egg mixture. It can also be used as a filling for other vegetables like zucchini and eggplant in tarts and pies. When cold, it makes a delicious salad.

1 Heat half of the oil in a roasting pan in an oven preheated to 425 degrees. Add the eggplant, zucchini, and peppers, toss in the hot oil, return to the oven and roast until tender, about 30 minutes.

2 While the vegetables are cooking, heat the rest of the oil in a deep saucepan and fry the onions and garlic until soft but not colored. Add the tomato paste, plum tomatoes, basil, marjoram or oregano, thyme, and paprika, and season with salt and pepper. Stir to combine and cook for 10–15 minutes until the mixture is thick and syrupy.

3 Using a slotted spoon, transfer the vegetables from the roasting pan to the tomato mixture. Gently stir to combine, then add the parsley and taste for seasoning. Serve hot or cold.

Serves 8–9

½ **cup olive oil**

2 large eggplant, quartered lengthwise and cut into ½ inch slices

2 zucchini, cut into ½ inch slices

2 large red bell peppers, cored, seeded, and cut into squares

1 large yellow pepper, cored, seeded, and cut into squares

2 large onions, thinly sliced

3 large garlic cloves, crushed

1 tablespoon double concentrate tomato paste

1 x 13-ounces can plum tomatoes

12 basil leaves, chopped

1 tablespoon finely chopped marjoram or oregano

1 teaspoon finely chopped thyme

1 tablespoon paprika

2–4 tablespoons minced parsley

salt and pepper

beef & carrot tzimmes
with thimble dumplings

This robust and hearty stew was inspired by the wonderful rich melting sweetness that fresh new carrots have when they are combined with syrup, a Jewish cookery technique. The syrup accentuates the flavor of the carrots and creates a partnership which, although sweet, is neither sickly nor cloying. In this recipe I have used equal quantities of beef and carrots; for a vegetarian alternative, substitute the meat with 3 cups strongly-flavored vegetables such as parsnips, turnip, celery root, celery, and potatoes.

1 Heat the oil in a large skillet. Add the meat a little at a time and fry to seal in the meat juices and brown the meat well on all sides. Do not add all the meat to the pan at once or the temperature of the oil will be reduced and the meat will not brown. Using a slotted spoon, transfer the meat to a large saucepan or flameproof casserole.

2 Fry the onion until beginning to color, drain, and add to the meat. Stir in the flour. Blend the syrup with a little of the warmed broth, then add to the pan with the rest of the broth, the carrots, bay leaf, and seasoning. Stir to combine and bring to a boil. Cover, reduce the heat, and simmer gently for 1–1½ hours until the meat is almost tender.

3 Meanwhile, make the thimble dumplings. Rub the butter into the flour until the mixture resembles fine bread crumbs. Stir in the parsley and thyme and season with salt and pepper. Make a well in the center, beat the egg and 2 tablespoons water together and pour into the well. Mix to a sticky dough, adding a little extra water if necessary.

4 About 20–30 minutes before the end of the cooking time for the stew, drop small teaspoonfuls of the dough on to the simmering stew. Cover and cook until the dumplings are risen, light and fluffy and the meat and vegetables are tender. Sprinkle with parsley and serve.

Serves 4

2–3 tablespoons sunflower oil
1½ pounds braising or stewing beef, such as chuck steak, topside or thick plate, cut into 1 inch slices
1 large onion, chopped
2 tablespoons all-purpose flour
1–2 tablespoons dark corn syrup
3 cups beef broth
1½ pounds carrots, cut into 1 inch chunks
1 bay leaf
salt and pepper
2 tablespoons minced parsley, to garnish

Thimble Dumplings:
4 tablespoons butter
1 cup self-rising flour
2 tablespoons minced parsley
pinch of fresh thyme
1 small egg
2–3 tablespoons cold water

pumpkin & root vegetable stew

This rich stew is substantial and filling. Serve it with Cheese-flavored Leek & Herb Scones (page 240), or with crusty bread or garlic mashed potatoes for a main course or supper dish. It will keep for 2–3 days in the refrigerator and actually improves with time, like most stews. Any leftovers can be turned into a gratin with the addition of thick cream and a topping of browned bread crumbs, and grated cheese.

1 Cut the pumpkin or squash in half across its widest part and remove and discard the seeds and stringy flesh. Cut into sections like a melon, then into cubes, removing the skin. You should have about 2 pounds or 4 cups flesh. Take care when cutting the skin because it is tough and the knife can easily slip.

2 Heat the oil in a large saucepan or flameproof casserole and fry the onion, garlic and chili until soft but not colored. Add the pumpkin and celery and fry gently for 10 minutes. Stir in the carrots, parsnip, tomatoes, tomato paste, paprika, broth, and bouquet garni. Bring to a boil, then reduce the heat, cover and simmer for 1–1½ hours until the vegetables are almost tender.

3 Add the beans and cook for 10 minutes. Season with salt and pepper and sprinkle with the chopped parsley before serving.

Serves 8–10

6 cups pumpkin or squash

3 tablespoons sunflower or olive oil

1 large onion, minced

3–4 garlic cloves, crushed

1 small red chili pepper, seeded and chopped

4 celery sticks, cut into 1 inch lengths

10 ounces carrots, cut into 1 inch chunks

1 parsnip, cut into 1 inch chunks

2 x 13-ounce cans plum tomatoes

2 tablespoons tomato paste

1 tablespoon hot paprika

⅔–1¼ cups light vegetable broth

1 bouquet garni

2 x 13-ounce cans red kidney beans, drained

salt and pepper

3–4 tablespoons minced parsley, to garnish

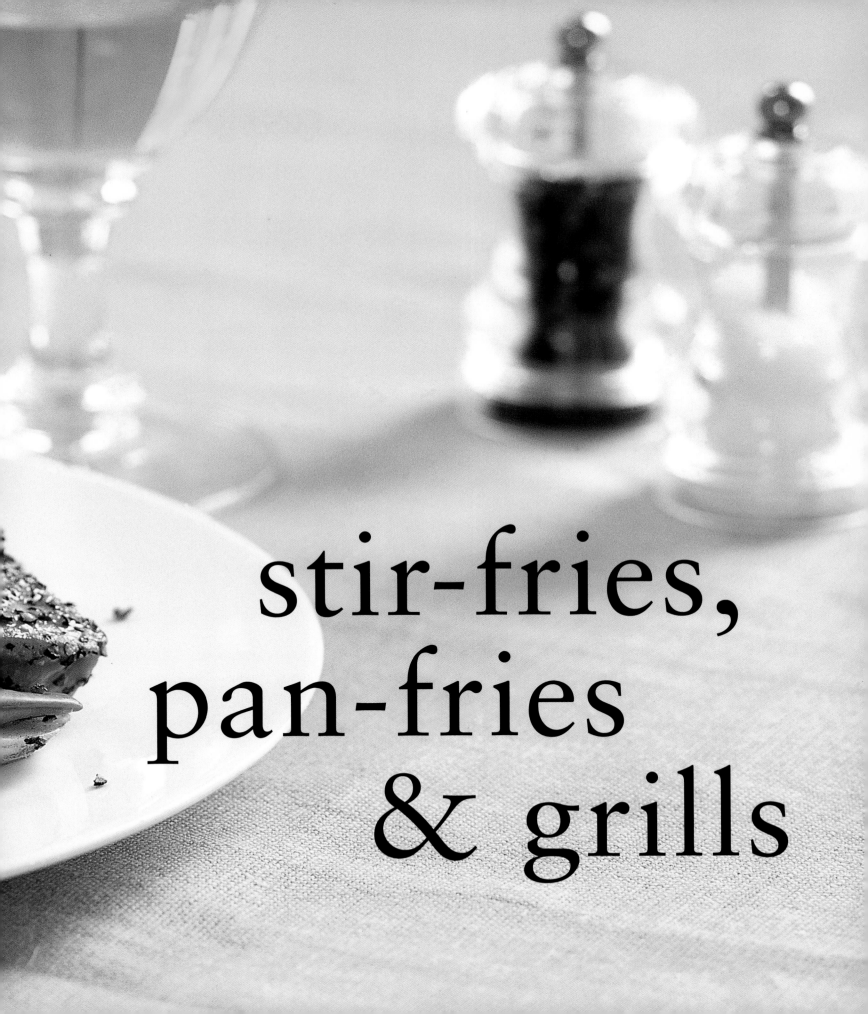

stir-fries,
pan-fries
& grills

peppered tuna steaks
with fennel, red onions, & sugar snaps

4 tablespoons black peppercorns

1 teaspoon salt

4 trimmed tuna steaks, each weighing 4–5 ounces, cut from the middle section of the fish

1 tablespoon olive oil

4 tablespoons cognac

⅔ cup concentrated fish or chicken broth

juice of 1 small lemon

4 tablespoons unsalted butter, cut into small dice

⅔ cup heavy cream

2 tablespoons minced parsley

4 flat leaf parsley sprigs, to garnish

Vegetables:

2 fennel bulbs

2 red onions

½ cup sugar snap peas or snowpeas

4 potatoes

2 tablespoons olive oil

2 tablespoons unsalted butter

1 First prepare the vegetables. Remove the feathery fronds from the fennel bulbs, chop finely, and reserve. Trim the root ends off the fennel and discard. Cut the fennel in half lengthwise and cut into ¼ inch thick slices. Cut the onions into rings. Top and tail the sugar snap peas or snowpeas and cut in half lengthwise on the diagonal. Peel the potatoes.

2 Heat the oil and butter in a large skillet, fry the fennel gently for 5 minutes, then add the onions. Cook over a moderate heat until the fennel and onions are tender, then increase the heat to color slightly. Remove from the heat and keep warm. Boil the potatoes until just tender.

3 Meanwhile, coarsely crush the peppercorns with a pestle or the end of a rolling pin. Mix with the salt. Brush the tuna with the olive oil and press in the pepper mixture to coat them. Heat a large skillet over a moderate heat. Set the steaks in the dry pan and fry for 2 minutes on one side, then turn and sauté for 1 minute on the second side.

4 Add the sugar snap peas or snowpeas to the fennel and onion mixture along with the fennel fronds and toss over a high heat until hot. Drain the potatoes, cut each one into 4–5 slices, and keep warm. Transfer the tuna to a warmed dish and keep warm.

5 Turn the heat up under the skillet. Add any remaining cracked pepper, pour on the cognac and a little of the broth, and stir to scrape up the sediment and any fish juices. Let the mixture bubble fiercely for a few seconds, then add the rest of the broth and the lemon juice and boil rapidly until syrupy.

6 Remove the skillet from the heat and gradually add the butter pieces, stirring to combine them with the sauce and thicken it. Add the cream, still stirring to mix well. Bring to a boil for a few seconds, add the chopped parsley and reduce the heat. Keep warm while serving the fish.

7 Divide the vegetables between 4 warm plates, arranging them in a mound in the center. Set a tuna steak on top of this and pour a little of the peppered sauce on top of each steak and around the edge of the vegetables. Garnish each with a sprig of flat leaf parsley and serve immediately.

Serves 4

Peppered Tuna Steaks are shown on the preceding page

corn & tofu
burgers with spiked yogurt sauce

Tofu, or bean curd as it is also known, is one of the mainstays of oriental vegetarian cuisine because of its high nutritional value. It is an important source of protein, contains very little saturated fat, and no cholesterol. It also provides a supply of calcium which compares well to dairy milk and contains B vitamins, niacin, phosphorus, sodium, and iron. These tofu burgers can be made with finely chopped roasted red pepper added to the mixture along with 1 teaspoon sweet chili pepper sauce. They are also good served with a rich tomato or tomato and pepper sauce instead of the yogurt sauce. Formed into tiny rounds, they make an excellent hot or cold cocktail savory.

1 Heat 2 tablespoons oil and fry the onion and garlic until soft but not colored. Put the tofu in a bowl and mash with a fork. Stir in the onion and garlic. Add the corn, half of the bread crumbs, the parsley, and basil. Mix the broth granules with the soy sauce and beaten egg and add to the other ingredients. Stir to combine and season to taste.

2 Divide the mixture into 8 equal pieces. Shape into patties, toss in the remaining bread crumbs, and fry gently in a little hot oil until golden-brown. They will take about 5–8 minutes on each side.

3 Meanwhile, make the sauce. Heat the oil and fry the garlic, mustard seeds, and ginger for 3–4 minutes until coloring. Set aside to cool. Put the yogurt into a bowl, add the garlic mixture, and season with salt and pepper. Stir to combine. Dust with the cayenne pepper, cover and chill.

4 Drain the cooked burgers on paper towels. Serve hot, with the yogurt sauce and a mixed leaf salad.

Serves 4–6

sunflower oil, for frying
¾ cup minced onion
1 garlic clove, crushed
¾ cup firm tofu, drained
1 x cup canned corn, drained
3 cups whole-wheat
  bread crumbs
3 tablespoons minced parsley
1 teaspoon minced basil
1 tablespoon broth granules
1 tablespoon soy sauce
1 small egg, beaten
salt and pepper

Spiked Yogurt Sauce:
1 tablespoon sunflower oil
1 garlic clove, minced
1 tablespoon black mustard seeds
1 teaspoon grated fresh root ginger
1 cup thick plain yogurt
pinch of cayenne pepper

corn &
red pepper frittata

Frittata is Italy's version of the omelet: flat, round, completely set through although still moist, and generally about two fingers thick. It is perfect served warm as a light lunch or supper dish with salad, or as part of a composed salad plate or a cocktail savory. It is also good served cold, and is ideal for picnics because it travels so well.

1 Heat the oil and fry the onion, garlic, and celery until soft but not colored. Stir in the red pepper and continue to cook until soft and beginning to color. Set aside to cool.

2 Break the eggs into a bowl and mix with the milk until just blended, using a fork. Transfer the cooked vegetables to the eggs with a slotted spoon, leaving behind any excess oil. Stir in the corn, parsley, bread crumbs, and half of the Parmesan. Season well.

3 Put the butter into a 6-inch omelet pan and heat until foaming but not brown. Pour the frittata mixture into the pan, stirring with a fork while pouring to disperse the vegetables. The pan will be almost full. Stop stirring, turn the heat down to very low, and cook for about 5–10 minutes. The eggs should be set with only the top surface runny.

4 Sprinkle the remaining Parmesan on top of the frittata and slide the pan under a preheated broiler for about 1 minute, just long enough to set the top and color the cheese slightly. Leave to rest for a few minutes before sliding out on to a board or plate and cutting into wedges, fingers, or cubes. Serve garnished with arugula leaves.

Serves 4 as a main course, 8 as a light snack

Makes ¾ inch cubes as a cocktail savory

2–3 tablespoons light olive oil

I onion, minced

2 garlic cloves, crushed

I celery stick, finely chopped

I red pepper, cored, seeded, and finely diced

5 large eggs

2 tablespoons milk

I x 7-ounce can corn, drained

3 tablespoons minced parsley

2–3 tablespoons fine white fresh bread crumbs

4 tablespoons grated Parmesan cheese

2 tablespoons unsalted butter

salt and pepper

arugula leaves, to garnish

wild mushroom omelet

This recipe uses one of my favorite fall mushrooms, chanterelles. You can of course use any variety of mushrooms. If using dried mushrooms, soak them for about 30 minutes before draining, chopping, and frying.

1 First prepare the filling. In a small pan (not the omelet pan), melt two-thirds of the butter and fry the mushrooms until soft and slightly colored, but still holding their shape. Stir in the herbs, flour, and cream, season with salt and pepper, and cook for a few minutes. Remove from the heat and keep warm.

2 Break the eggs into a shallow dish (such as a soup plate.) Add salt, pepper, and half of the remaining butter. Beat the eggs lightly with a fork, just enough to combine. Warm an 8-inch omelet pan, then put in the remaining butter. When it begins to foam and just before it starts to brown, pour in the eggs. Quickly stir the contents of the pan 2–3 times with the flat of the fork so that as much of the mixture as possible is exposed to the heat.

3 When the underside of the omelet has begun to set, pull the edge of the omelet into the center with the fork and tilt the pan at the same time so that the liquid egg can flow towards the hot surface and set. The omelet is cooked when the underside is set but the top is still soft and slightly runny.

4 Spread the filling over the omelet, folding the nearest edge of the omelet into the center using a fork or metal spatula. Tilt the pan away from you, slip the fork under the fold, and tip the omelet over again, rolling it toward the edge of the pan. Pull the last remaining bit of omelet from the far edge of the pan over the folded section and press down gently to seal. Keep the tilted pan over the heat for a few seconds to brown the bottom of the omelet slightly.

5 Tip the pan against the plate, holding it in such a way that it rolls golden-side uppermost on to the plate. Draw a small piece of butter over the surface of the omelet to give it a sheen, then serve immediately.

Serves 1

3 tablespoons unsalted butter, cut into small cubes
1 cup mushrooms, brushed or wiped, trimmed, and finely sliced
1 teaspoon minced herbs (parsley, chives, chervil)
pinch of all-purpose flour
1–2 tablespoons heavy cream
3 large eggs
salt and pepper

alternative omelet fillings

Eggplant or Zucchini Cut into matchstick pieces about 1½ inches long and fry in hot oil for 3–4 minutes. Drain and scatter over the omelet in the pan.

Avocado Finely dice avocado flesh and scatter over the omelet in the pan.

Grilled Sweet Red Pepper Finely shred grilled red bell pepper and add to the omelet in the pan.

Mixed Herbs Add 1 tablespoon finely chopped mixed herbs (equal quantities of flat leaf parsley, chervil, and chives with a pinch of tarragon) to the beaten eggs. Or add shredded basil leaves and a little marjoram to the beaten eggs.

Ratatouille Heat 4–6 tablespoons of prepared Ratatouille (page 162) and spread over the omelet in the pan.

Shallots or Garlic Cook finely sliced shallots or garlic in oil and scatter over the omelet in the pan.

Sorrel or Watercress Finely shred a handful of tender young sorrel leaves and add to the omelet in the pan to give a wonderful sharp, sour taste. Watercress leaves used in the same way give a peppery bite.

Tomato Toss peeled, seeded, and diced tomato in a little butter, season, and strew across the omelet in the pan.

stir-fried duck
with ginger & vegetables

Because duck breast, like chicken breast, is so tender, it requires very little cooking and lends itself particularly well to stir-frying. I devised this recipe for my friends Lilla and Ronnie Steel of Silver Hill Duckling in Monaghan, Ireland. It goes well with boiled rice, egg-fried rice, or noodles.

1 Cut the duck into finger-thick strips. Halve the peppers lengthwise and remove the seeds and white parts. Cut into strips about 1½ inches long and ⅛ inch thick. Peel and cut the carrot to a similar size and shape. Peel the ginger and cut into very thin pieces. Trim the green onions (scallions) and cut into 1½ inch lengths.

2 Combine all the ingredients for the sauce in a large measuring cup.

3 Heat the oil in a wok or large skillet and stir-fry the duck quickly until just beginning to color. This should take about 3 minutes. Add all of the vegetables and continue to stir-fry for a further few minutes, tossing everything together in the pan.

4 Stir the sauce to make sure it is well blended, then pour into the pan. Bring to a boil and cook for a few minutes, stirring all the time to combine the flavors while the sauce is cooking and thickening. Serve immediately.

Serves 4

2 boneless, skinless duck breasts, total weight about 1 pound
2 bell peppers, 1 red, 1 green
1 large carrot
½ inch piece of fresh root ginger
8 green onions (scallions)
2 tablespoons sunflower oil
½ cup beansprouts

Sauce:
2 garlic cloves, crushed
2 tablespoons cornstarch
1 tablespoon Szechuan seasoning
2 tablespoons dark soft brown sugar
1 teaspoon ground ginger
4 tablespoons soy sauce
2 tablespoons sherry
2½ cups chicken, duck, or vegetable broth

red lentil burgers
spiked with chili peppers and garlic

Among the vegetable cook's great resources are lentils. They are inexpensive, versatile, and nutritious, rich in protein, carbohydrates, vitamins, and iron. Unlike beans, they don't require long soaking and cooking, and bright orange, red, or yellow lentils, either whole or split, can be quickly cooked to a thick purée which forms the basis of many dishes. Because they are without a strong taste of their own, they combine perfectly with rich powerful flavors. Serve these burgers with thick plain yogurt or Cucumber & Mint Raita (page 216) and a mixed leaf salad.

1 Wash the lentils and put them into a large saucepan of boiling water. Return to a boil, then reduce the heat to a simmer. Cook gently for 20–40 minutes until the lentils are pulpy, the liquid has evaporated, and the mixture is dry in texture. Stir frequently during cooking to ensure that the lentils do not burn. Spread the cooked lentils on a cookie sheet and set aside to cool.

2 Meanwhile, heat the sunflower oil and fry the onion, garlic, red pepper, and chili pepper until soft but not colored. Set aside to cool.

3 In a large bowl, combine the lentils, onion mixture, 1 cup of the bread crumbs, the Cheddar cheese, tomato paste, parsley, and broth granules. Stir well, season and add the beaten egg, then mix to combine.

4 Divide the mixture into 12 pieces. Dip them in the remaining bread crumbs and make into burgers about 3 inches in diameter. Heat a little oil in a large skillet and fry the burgers for about 5–6 minutes until very hot all the way through and brown on both sides. Drain on paper towels and serve hot.

Makes 12 burgers, enough to serve 6

1 cup split red lentils

3 cups boiling water

3 tablespoons sunflower oil

1 large onion, minced

2–3 garlic cloves, finely chopped

1 large red bell pepper, seeded and finely chopped

1–2 small red chili peppers, seeded and finely chopped

2 cups fresh white bread crumbs

⅔ cup mature Cheddar cheese, grated

1 tablespoon tomato paste

3 tablespoons finely chopped parsley

½ teaspoon broth granules

1 small egg, beaten

vegetable oil, for frying

salt and pepper

Spanish potato omelet

This thick, juicy, fragrant omelet, known as tortilla *in Spain, is made from eggs, onions and potatoes. It is served hot (though more generally warm) or cold, as a first course, main course, light supper or snack, and is both delicious and satisfying. Cut into wedges, it is served on its own or accompanied by fried eggs, sausages, bacon or peppers.*

1 Heat the oil in a 8–9 inch heavy nonstick skillet. Add the slices of potato one at a time, then alternate layers of potato with layers of onion slices. Cover the pan and cook the onion and potatoes over a low heat without coloring until the potatoes are tender, lifting and turning them occasionally. This will take about 30–45 minutes. At this stage the potatoes will remain separate; they will not have formed a "cake."

2 Beat the eggs with a fork in a large bowl until they are slightly foamy. Season with salt and pepper. Once the vegetables are soft and well cooked, lift them out of the pan with a slotted spoon and drain them in a colander. Reserve the oil for frying the tortilla. Add the potatoes and onions to the beaten eggs, pressing them well down so that they are completely immersed. If possible, leave to stand for about 15 minutes.

3 Wipe the pan clean, then heat about 2–3 tablespoons of the reserved oil. Add the egg mixture and quickly spread it out with a metal spatula. Reduce the heat and cook very gently, shaking the pan occasionally to prevent it from sticking. When the potatoes begin to brown underneath and shrink slightly from the edge of the pan after about 15 minutes, remove the pan from the heat.

4 Turn the tortilla over by placing a flat plate, slightly larger than the pan, on top of it, and quickly turn the tortilla upside down on to the plate. Don't worry if the omelet sticks slightly to the pan when you turn it over, just remove the pieces and press them back into the omelet.

5 Heat another tablespoon of oil in the pan, then slide the tortilla back to brown the other side. This will take another 3–4 minutes. Alternatively, instead of turning the tortilla, just slip the pan under a preheated moderate grill and cook until the surface is golden brown. The tortilla should be golden brown on the outside and moist and juicy inside. Transfer to a plate or board and serve hot or cold.

Serves 4–6 as an entrée

⅔ **cup olive oil**
4 large potatoes, cut into
 ⅛ **inch slices**
1 large onion, thinly sliced
4–5 large eggs
salt and pepper

salmon & Zucchini brochettes

These kabobs are shown on a bed of arugula with Lime & Sesame Dressing (page 231). They are equally delicious served on mashed potatoes flavored with olive oil, with the salad served separately. They can also be made with fresh tuna or swordfish.

1 You will need 8 barbecue skewers. If they are wooden, put them to soak in cold water. Prepare the marinade by combining all the ingredients in a large bowl. Add the salmon and zucchini pieces and toss to combine and coat. Cover and leave to marinate for about 30 minutes.

2 Thread the salmon and zucchini pieces alternately on to the barbecue skewers and cook the kabobs under a preheated very hot broiler or over a very hot barbecue for about 5 minutes, turning them frequently and brushing with the marinade to keep the fish and zucchini from drying out. The fish is cooked when it is just beginning to look milky. Take care not to overcook it or it will become dry and tough. Serve immediately on a bed of arugula, garnished with whole chives and lime wedges.

Serves 4

**1½–2 pounds salmon fillet, skinned
and cut into 1 inch cubes**
**4 zucchini, cut into
½ inch pieces**

Marinade:
8 tablespoons sunflower oil
2 tablespoons light sesame seed oil
2 tablespoons sesame seeds
1 garlic clove, crushed
1–2 tablespoons lime juice
pepper

To Serve:
arugula
whole chives
lime wedges

vegetable brochettes
with mustard & herb glaze

These brochettes, a collection of seasonal mixed vegetables grilled over a wood or charcoal fire or broiled under an electric or gas broiler, are colorful and delicious at any time of the year. Choose vegetables with firm moist flesh that will cook quickly without disintegrating; and partially pre-cook resilient vegetables like potatoes, yams (yucca), and onions. This will ensure that delicate items aren't cooked to a frazzled mush while others remain inedible. I generally allow 1 cup mixed vegetables per person.

1 Plunge the pickling onions into boiling water and blanch for 2–3 minutes. Refresh under cold water, drain and peel. Cut the pepper in half lengthwise, remove the seeds and cut the flesh into 1 inch squares or wedges. Slice eggplant into ¼ inch rounds or cut baby ones in half lengthwise. Cut zucchini into ¾ inch rounds and blanch for 1 minute. Cut corn-on-the-cob into ½ inch rounds and cook in boiling water for 2–3 minutes. Refresh and drain. Trim fennel at the root to free the leaves and cut each bulb into 1 inch pieces.

2 Arrange the vegetables in bowls on a tray. If using wooden skewers, soak them in cold water. Place a mushroom or onion at the ends of each skewer to anchor the other vegetables, then thread an assortment on each one to make a colorful and attractive display. Put the prepared brochettes on the tray.

3 Combine all the ingredients for the glaze in a bowl. Brush this generously over the brochettes, turning them so they are well coated. Cover with plastic wrap and refrigerate until required, along with the remaining glaze. These can be prepared several hours in advance.

4 Broil the brochettes under a preheated broiler or over a barbecue, turning them every few minutes to expose all surfaces to the heat and brushing with extra marinade as required. When the vegetables are cooked, sizzling hot and nicely browned, serve immediately with skewers of grilled chili pepper-flavored new potatoes, a choice of salads and toasted pita bread.

Serves 4

12 pickling onions
1 large red, green, or yellow
  bell pepper
2 or 3 vegetables, such as eggplant,
  zucchini, corn-on-the-cob, or
  fennel bulbs
24 button mushrooms, wiped

Mustard & Herb Glaze:
2 tablespoons Dijon mustard
2 tablespoons finely chopped mixed
  herbs (parsley, thyme, marjoram,
  basil)
2 garlic cloves, crushed
4 tablespoons red wine vinegar
½–1 teaspoon sweet chili pepper
  sauce
2 teaspoons clear honey
salt and pepper

mushroom
& tofu kabobs

This recipe was inspired by one of my favorite sauces, satay sauce, the rich and spicy nutty concoction from Indonesia that is traditionally served with strips of marinated chicken. If you want a more "meaty" kabob, add cubes of chicken breast to the marinade along with the tofu and mushrooms. For an entrée, serve with white basmati rice.

1 cup firm tofu
36 even-sized, firm button mushrooms

Marinade:
3 tablespoons sunflower oil
3 garlic cloves, crushed
3 teaspoons ground coriander
3 teaspoons ground cumin
4–6 tablespoons clear honey
3 tablespoons sweet chili pepper sauce
4 tablespoons tamari or soy sauce
8 tablespoons cold water
4 tablespoons lime juice

To Garnish:
coriander (cilantro) sprigs
Indonesian Peanut Dipping Sauce (page 224)

1 First make the marinade. Heat the oil in a small saucepan and fry the garlic over a low heat until soft but not colored. Stir in the dry spices and fry for a few minutes to develop the flavors. Remove from the heat and stir in the honey, chili pepper, and tamari or soy sauces, water, and lime juice. Bring to a boil and cook for a few minutes to blend the flavors, then remove from the heat and leave to cool.

2 Drain the tofu and cut it into ¾ inch cubes. Wipe the mushrooms and trim the stalks level with the caps if long. Set the tofu and mushrooms in a single layer in a large, shallow non-metallic dish. Soak twelve 8-inch fine bamboo skewers in cold water.

3 Pour the cool marinade over the tofu and mushrooms, cover and leave for about 1 hour to marinate.

4 Thread the tofu and mushrooms alternately on the soaked skewers. Place under a preheated grill or on a barbecue and brush all over with the marinade. Cook for 8–10 minutes, turning and basting frequently until browned.

5 Serve the kabobs hot, garnished with coriander (cilantro) sprigs. Hand the Indonesian Peanut Dipping Sauce separately.

Serves 4 as a main course, 6 as a first course

wilted greens
with water chestnuts & black bean sauce

Oriental cooking, with its quick stir-fry technique and imaginative flavor combinations, offers the perfect example of how leafy greens can be used to create interestingly textured dishes. In this recipe, I have combined the delicate leaves of bok choy with crisp broccoli, but any leafy green cabbage can be used. They are quickly stir-fried before being enriched with a black bean sauce, a hint of chili pepper and toasted sesame seeds – a delicious main course served with rice or noodles.

1 First prepare the sauce. Put the cornstarch into a bowl, gradually add about 2 tablespoons of the broth, and mix to a smooth paste. Stir in the rest of the ingredients and season to taste. Set aside until required.

2 Shred the bok choy, but not too finely. Trim any woody stems from the broccoli and divide the head into flowerets each with a little stem.

3 Heat the sunflower and sesame oils in a large wok or pan, add the onion and garlic and stir-fry until soft but not colored. Increase the heat, add the bok choy, broccoli and water-chestnuts and stir-fry over a high heat for about 3–5 minutes until the vegetables are almost tender. Add the beansprouts. Stir the sauce and add to the pan, tossing the vegetables in it to coat thoroughly. Bring to a boil and cook for about 1 minute to thicken the sauce. Taste for seasoning, sprinkle with the toasted sesame seeds, and serve immediately.

Serves 4

Black Bean Sauce:
- **1 tablespoon cornstarch**
- **1¼ cups vegetable broth**
- **2–4 tablespoons soy sauce**
- **2 tablespoons black bean sauce**
- **2 teaspoons sweet chili pepper sauce**
- **1 tablespoon clear honey**
- **salt and pepper**

Wilted Greens:
- **1 pound bok choy**
- **2 cups broccoli flowerets**
- **3 tablespoons sunflower oil**
- **1 tablespoon light sesame oil**
- **1 onion, quartered and thinly sliced**
- **3 garlic cloves, thinly sliced**
- **1 x 8-ounce can water-chestnuts, drained and sliced**
- **¼–½ cup beansprouts**
- **2 tablespoons sesame seeds, toasted**

stir-fried noodles with
broccoli, corn, beansprouts, & smoked tofu

In this recipe I have combined dried thread egg noodles and smoked tofu with crisp broccoli, corn, and beansprouts to create an interesting variety of flavor, texture, and color. Any crunchy vegetables, such as snowpeas, sugar snap peas, water-chestnuts, or asparagus, could be used. All the preparation can be done in advance and the ingredients stored in the refrigerator for up to 8 hours until required. The cooking, like all stir-frying, only takes a few minutes. Serve with Pickled Cucumber (page 249.)

1 Cook the noodles in a large pan of boiling water according to package instructions until just tender. Drain and refresh under cold running water until very cold. Leave to drain.

2 Heat about 2 inches sunflower oil in a wok or heavy-based skillet and fry the tofu cubes for 3–4 minutes until crisp and lightly golden. Drain on paper towels and keep warm.

3 Remove all but a few tablespoons of the oil from the wok and fry the onion, ginger, garlic, and chili pepper until soft but not brown. Remove from the heat.

4 Blanch the broccoli in a large saucepan of boiling water for about 1 minute, drain and refresh under cold water until absolutely cold. Drain again and pat dry with paper towels.

5 Combine all the ingredients for the sauce in a bowl and mix well.

6 Return the wok or pan with the onion mixture to the heat. When reheated, add the broccoli and stir-fry for 2–3 minutes. Add the corn and beansprouts and stir-fry for about 3 minutes, keeping the ingredients moving. Add the sauce, toss to combine, then add the noodles and the fried tofu. Cook for another 1 minute until everything is heated through.

Serves 4

6 ounces dried thread egg noodles
sunflower oil, for frying
1 cup firm smoked tofu, cubed
1 onion, minced
1 teaspoon grated fresh root ginger
2 garlic cloves, crushed
1 small red chili pepper, seeded and
  finely sliced
1 cup broccoli flowerets
¾ cup baby corn, cut in half
  lengthwise
¾ cup fresh beansprouts

Sauce:
1 cup teriyaki sauce
2 tablespoons sake (Japanese rice
  wine)
2 tablespoons lemon juice
2–3 teaspoons sweet chili
  pepper sauce
2 teaspoons brown sugar

crisp green vegetables
stir-fried with mushrooms in sweet-&-sour sauce

2 tablespoons sunflower oil

2 garlic cloves, crushed

1 onion, thinly sliced

2 inch piece of fresh root
ginger, peeled and thinly sliced

½ cup mushrooms, sliced

1 green pepper, cored, seeded, and
cut into strips

½ cup green beans, cut in half

½ cup snowpeas or sugar snap peas,
left whole, cut in half or into three
diagonally

¾ cup broccoli, trimmed, cut into
bite-sized flowerets and stalks
peeled

2 sticks celery, cut into thin
1½ inch lengths

6 green onions (scallions), cut into
thin 1½ inch lengths

salt and pepper

Sweet & Sour Sauce:

1 tablespoon cornstarch

3 tablespoons soy sauce

2 tablespoons sweet chili pepper
sauce

1 teaspoon oyster sauce

2 tablespoons rice wine or sherry

4 tablespoons water

2 tablespoons sunflower oil

2 tablespoons dark soft brown sugar

Stir-frying is one of the best ways of cooking vegetables to retain their color, crispness and much of their food value. This recipe is particularly versatile because any crisp vegetables can be used. Good vegetables to choose from are firm ones such as celery, peppers, fennel, broccoli, and cauliflower flowerets, leeks, snowpeas, sugar snaps, green beans, zucchini, and green onions (scallions.) Serve with rice or noodles.

1 First combine all the ingredients for the sauce in a measuring cup or bowl. Set aside.

2 Heat a wok, then add the oil. When it is hot, add the garlic, onion and ginger and stir-fry until soft but not colored. Add the mushrooms, tossing quickly. Add the remaining vegetables and stir-fry for a further few minutes until tender but still bright in color and crisp.

3 Pour on the sauce, tossing and turning the ingredients in the wok. Season to taste and serve immediately.

Serves 4–6

broiled vegetables
with dipping sauce

The simple technique of broiling vegetables intensifies their succulence and flavor. As the flesh softens and the juices run, they caramelize, causing the skin to wrinkle, and char and produce that incomparable depth of flavor. Broiled vegetables can also be served with salad leaves, drizzled with olive oil, seasoned with pepper and scattered with Parmesan shavings — this makes an excellent light lunch or first course.

1 Put the garlic and olive oil in a bowl and leave to infuse while preparing the vegetables.

2 Slice the onion across into rings, discarding the ends. Try to keep the rings together. Place on a large plastic or metal tray. Slice the small fennel bulb through its length into about 3 flat slices or leave mini fennel whole.

3 Cut the peppers in half lengthwise and remove the seeds, white membranes and stalks. Cut in half again. Place the pepper wedges on the tray. Slice the eggplant in half lengthwise through the stalk if mini or small; if large, slice thinly from stalk to tip. With the point of a sharp knife, lightly score the flesh of the eggplant in a criss-cross fashion. Set beside the peppers. Top and tail the zucchini and cut in half lengthwise. Set on the tray.

4 Cut the endive in half lengthwise. Peel and remove the stalks from the mushrooms. Set on the tray. Brush each vegetable with the garlic-flavored oil.

5 Cook the vegetables on a very hot barbecue or ridged broiler pan, or on a preheated very hot heavy baking sheet under a preheated broiler. Start with the vegetables which take longest, gradually adding the rest until they are all done — onions and fennel take 10–20 minutes, peppers, eggplant, and zucchini 15 minutes, endive and mushrooms 5 minutes. Turn the vegetables during cooking and raise or lower the broiler pan as required. If using a ridged pan, press the vegetables against the hot surface with a metal spatula. When ready, the vegetables should be *al dente*, colored, and blistering.

6 Arrange the vegetables on a large platter, or individual plates and garnish with lemon and parsley. Offer extra-virgin olive oil separately, or any other sauce of your choice such as Pesto (page 234) or Salsa Verde (page 211). Serve warm, with crusty bread.

Serves 4

4 garlic cloves, finely chopped

10–12 tablespoons extra virgin olive oil

1 large red onion, peeled

4 mini fennel bulbs, or 1 small fennel bulb

2 large peppers (1 red, 1 yellow)

4 mini eggplant, or 2 small eggplant

4 baby zucchini, or 2 small zucchini

1 head endive

4 large field mushrooms

To Garnish:
1 large lemon, cut into wedges
flat leaf parsley sprigs

chicken with vegetables,
noodles & cashew nuts

Because the cooking time is so short, you need to have everything ready before you start cooking this dish. Pork or beef fillet or sirloin steak can be used instead of chicken.

1 First combine all the ingredients for the sauce in a bowl, gradually adding the broth to make a smooth liquid.

2 Combine the sunflower and sesame oils, heat half in a wok or large skillet and stir-fry the chicken strips until cooked. This will only take about 3 minutes. Remove from the pan. Add the remaining oil mixture and stir-fry the carrot for 1 minute, then add the peppers, snowpeas, and corn, constantly tossing and frying over a high heat.

3 Stir the sauce to make sure it is well blended, then pour it into the pan. Bring to a boil and cook for a few minutes, stirring all the time. Add the noodles and chicken and cook for a further few minutes to heat thoroughly.

4 Pile a generous helping in the center of 4 warmed plates and sprinkle over the cashew nuts, spring onions and a little of the sauce. Garnish with coriander (cilantro) and serve immediately.

Serves 4

4 tablespoons sunflower oil

1 tablespoon light sesame seed oil

1½ pounds skinless, boneless chicken breasts, cut into thin strips

1 large carrot, cut into thin strips

2 large bell peppers (1 red, 1 yellow), cored, seeded, and cut into thin strips

¾ cup snowpeas

6 ounces baby corn

12 ounces medium egg noodles, cooked and drained

¼ –½ cup cashew nuts, toasted

2 green onions (scallions), thinly sliced

coriander (cilantro) leaves, to garnish

Sauce:

1½ tablespoons cornstarch

3 garlic cloves, minced

2 teaspoons finely grated fresh root ginger

3 tablespoons dark soft brown sugar

6 tablespoons tamari sauce

1 teaspoon Tabasco sauce

2 cups chicken broth

roasts
& bakes

roast root vegetable tarte Tatin

This savory version of the classic sweet tarte Tatin was inspired by the natural caramelization of roasted root vegetables and the simplicity of the crisp pastry lid — or rather base — on to which the meltingly tender vegetables cling. Try serving it with a mixed leaf salad and a piquant yogurt sauce.

1 Heat the oil in a large heavy roasting pan and add the carrots, turnips, parsnips, shallots, and spices. Toss over a high heat until lightly colored. Place in a preheated 425 degree oven for 20 minutes, then add the garlic cloves and roast for 10 minutes. Add the leeks and continue roasting for a further 10 minutes or until the vegetables are tender and a rich brown color.

2 Meanwhile, cut the pastry into six 4½ inch circles. Cover and refrigerate until required.

3 Make the caramel. Melt the butter with the sugar, vinegar, and water in a heavy skillet. Bring to a boil, shaking the pan and stirring until the sugar dissolves, then let the mixture bubble until it turns a deep golden caramel. It will turn pink and frothy before it turns a rich gold. By this stage the liquid will have evaporated. Keep shaking the pan and drawing the spoon across the center to disperse the heat. Quickly pour into the center of six shallow 3-inch heavy pie pans, spreading it over their bases if you can. It may set immediately, but it will liquefy again in the oven.

4 Arrange the vegetables over the caramel, then place the pastry discs over them, tucking in the pastry edges so they lie on top of the vegetables inside the pans. Set on a heavy cookie sheet and bake for 10–15 minutes until the pastry is crisp, risen, and golden. Cool for a few minutes, then invert on to warmed plates, handling the tarts carefully as the hot juices may run out. Serve the tarts hot, pastry side down.

Serves 6

3 tablespoons olive oil

6 ounces carrots, cut into
   1 inch chunks

6 ounces turnips, cut into
   1 inch chunks

6 ounces parsnips, cut into
   1 inch chunks

6 ounces shallots, halved if large

1 teaspoon coriander (cilantro)
   seeds, finely ground

1 teaspoon fennel seeds, finely
   ground

4 garlic cloves, peeled

6 ounces leeks, cut into
   1 inch chunks

1 x 12-ounce package ready
   rolled puff pastry

Caramel:
3 teaspoons butter

3 tablespoons sugar

1 tablespoon red wine vinegar

2 tablespoons water

Roast Root Vegetable Tarte Tatin is shown on the preceding page

zucchini & red pepper tian

This vegetable gratin takes its name from the dish in which it is cooked, a shallow earthenware dish from Provence which is wider across the top than the bottom. This ensures that there is much more of the crispy gratin topping than filling. You can use any lightly cooked vegetable or combination of vegetables, such as steamed, boiled, or fried broccoli, cauliflower, zucchini, or leeks. Macaroni or other small pasta shapes are an excellent alternative to the rice. Strips of lightly fried or poached chicken breast meat can also be added. Serve with a mixed leaf salad and crusty garlic bread.

4–5 tablespoons olive or sunflower oil

1 large onion, finely chopped

2 garlic cloves, crushed

3 cups zucchini, cut into ¼–½ inch cubes

1 red pepper, cored, seeded and diced

2 tablespoons minced coriander (cilantro)

1–2 tablespoons ground coriander (cilantro)

⅓ cup long-grain rice

2 large eggs

4 tablespoons grated mature Cheddar cheese

4 tablespoons freshly grated Parmesan cheese

4 tablespoons fine white bread crumbs

salt and pepper

1 Heat 3 tablespoons of the oil in a large, heavy wide-based saucepan and fry the onion and garlic until soft but not colored. Add the rest of the oil, increase the heat, then add the zucchini, red bell pepper, and chopped coriander (cilantro.) Fry for 5–10 minutes, then stir in the ground coriander (cilantro) and fry for a few minutes to develop the flavor.

2 Meanwhile, cook the long-grain rice in a large pan of boiling salted water for 11 minutes, or according to the package instructions, until just tender. Drain the rice well. Beat the eggs in a large bowl, season with salt and pepper and then stir into the zucchini mixture. Add the rice and two-thirds of the Cheddar and Parmesan cheeses.

3 Lightly oil a 1 quart gratin dish about 2 inches deep and fill with the vegetable mixture. Mix the remaining cheese with the bread crumbs and scatter on top. Bake in a preheated 350 degree oven for 20–30 minutes, or until the mixture is set and the top is beginning to turn crisp and golden-brown. I generally broil the tian under a very hot broiler to speed up the process. Serve hot or cold.

Serves 4

roast fillet of salmon
with tomato & avocado compote

This is a wonderfully simple recipe for an elegant summer meal. It can be prepared in advance and takes just a few minutes to cook and assemble. I use the chef's method of frying and roasting for cooking the salmon, but it can of course be completely cooked in the pan or under the broiler, turning the fish once during cooking. I generally use a cast iron skillet with an ovenproof handle, which can be transferred directly to the oven.

1 First prepare the compote. Put the tomatoes, avocado, olive oil, and lime juice into a bowl and add a dash each of Worcestershire and Tabasco sauces. Add salt and pepper to taste, cover and refrigerate until required.

2 Brush a heavy skillet lightly with oil and warm over a high heat. Season the salmon fillets with salt and pepper, place flesh-side down in the pan, and cook over a high heat for 2 minutes to brown the flesh. The fish should have a seared appearance.

3 Carefully transfer the fish, skin-side down, to a lightly oiled cookie sheet. Transfer the cookie sheet to a preheated 475 degree oven, and cook for 7–9 minutes depending on thickness. To tell if the fish is cooked, take a peek inside the salmon by slightly opening the flesh with a metal spatula; if it is still a little pink, cook for a little longer. Don't forget, it will continue to cook after it has been removed from the oven.

4 Divide the compote between 4 large plates, arranging it in the center of each one. Shake the dressing, then drizzle it over and around the compote. Set a piece of salmon on each mound of compote, garnish with basil leaves and serve immediately.

Serves 4

½ tablespoon sunflower oil
4 x 5–6 ounce salmon filets, skin on
  but scaled
Fresh Basil Dressing (page 230)
4 basil leaves, to garnish
salt and pepper

Compote:
4 ripe tomatoes, peeled, seeded and
  cut into ¼ inch dice
1 large firm, ripe avocado, pitted,
  peeled and cut into ¼ inch dice
1–2 tablespoons extra virgin olive oil
4–5 tablespoons lime juice
dash of Worcestershire sauce
dash of Tabasco sauce

carrot, mushroom
& mixed nut roast

This rich vegetable and mixed nut roast spiked with herbs and flavorings is moist and succulent. I make it in a large tube pan because this way it cuts into perfect slices. It also looks good on a festive or buffet table, the center filled with fresh watercress, tender young salad leaves, or a vegetable such as Brussels sprouts, mixed green beans, broccoli flowerets, or roasted baby beets. It can, of course, also be made in a large loaf pan or individual pans or molds. Any combination of nuts and vegetables can be used with carrot as the principal character. It is excellent hot or cold and is perfect with Spicy Tomato Sauce (page 232).

1 Lightly oil a 9½ inch tube pan or eight 4-inch individual tube pans. Line carefully with aluminum foil, taking care to smooth out any folds or wrinkles. Oil lightly.

2 Heat the oil and sauté the onion, celery, and garlic until soft. Add the mushrooms and fry until the color changes. Stir in the carrots and cook for a further 5 minutes.

3 Meanwhile, combine all the nuts in a food processor and process until finely chopped but still with a texture, or chop by hand. Put them into a large bowl with the bread crumbs, lemon rind, marjoram, parsley, mace, and thyme, and season with salt and pepper. Add the onion mixture and the eggs and broth or water. Mix well to blend and check the seasoning.

4 Pack the mixture into the mold or molds, smooth the top, and make sure there are no air spaces. Cover with oiled foil. Set on a heavy cookie sheet and bake in a preheated 375 degree oven, until firm to the touch. This will take 1½ hours for the large mold or 45 minutes for the small ones.

5 When cooked, remove the aluminum foil at the base and carefully invert the nut roast on to a warm serving dish or warmed individual plates. Remove the remaining aluminum foil and serve hot or cold.

Gives about 30 slices, enough to serve 8

2 tablespoons olive or sunflower oil
1 onion, about 6 ounces, minced
1 celery stick, finely chopped
1 garlic clove, minced
2 cups mushrooms, finely chopped
6 ounces carrots, grated
1 cup canned chestnuts, whole and peeled
1 cup hazelnuts, walnuts, peanuts, Brazil nuts, or pecan nuts
2 cups fine whole-wheat bread crumbs
1 teaspoon grated lemon rind
1 teaspoon finely chopped marjoram
2 tablespoons finely chopped parsley
1 teaspoon ground mace
pinch of dried thyme
3 large eggs, beaten
⅔ cup vegetable broth or water
salt and pepper

zucchini, tomato, & basil tart

A crisp melting pastry case filled with a single vegetable or a mixture of vegetables and set in a light custard is one of the classic dishes of any culinary repertoire. Here I have combined three of the summer garden's best — baby zucchini, flavorsome tomatoes and sweet basil. For mixed vegetable tarts, use whatever vegetables you fancy. Each tart needs 1¼ cups vegetables — or ⅓ cup for individual tartlets. One of my favorite combinations is onion, red and green bell pepper, zucchini, and tomato, all finely chopped and cooked in a little hot oil until soft. The custard mixture and pastry quantity remain the same. One of the secrets of success is that the pastry should be rolled out thinly — no more than ⅛ inch thick. Serve warm or cold.

1 First make the pastry. Sift the flour and salt into a bowl. Cut the fats into small pieces and coat with the flour. Rub the fat into the flour until it resembles fine bread crumbs. Mix together the egg yolk and water. Make a well in the center of the flour and add the liquid. Mix with a broad-bladed knife to form a stiff dough, adding a little extra water if necessary. Place in a plastic bag and chill for about 30 minutes.

2 For the large tart, roll the pastry into 1 large circle to line a 8 x 1½ inch tart pan. For tartlets, divide the pastry into quarters and roll out into circles just larger than four 4½ x ¾ inch tartlet pans, allowing just enough to cover the base and sides. Press the pastry against the sides of the pan or pans, keeping it an even thickness all the way round. Cut off any excess pastry with a knife. Prick the pastry base gently with a fork, line with foil and fill with baking beans. Set on a cookie sheet and bake blind in a preheated 400 degree oven for 8–10 minutes. Remove the baking beans and foil and bake for a further 8–10 minutes.

3 While the pastry is baking, make the filling. Heat the oil and fry the onion until soft but not colored, then stir in the chopped tomato and basil.

4 Spoon the filling into the cooked tart or tartlet shells and arrange the zucchini slices decoratively on top. Reduce the oven temperature to 350 degrees. Beat the eggs and cream together, add salt and pepper and pour over the filling. Sprinkle with grated Cheddar cheese and bake for 25–30 minutes for the large tart, 20–25 minutes for the tartlets, until just set and light golden.

Serves 4

1–2 tablespoons olive oil
1 onion, finely chopped
1 large tomato, peeled, seeded and chopped
4 basil leaves, finely chopped
8 tiny zucchini, cut into wafer-thin slices
2 large eggs
⅔ cup heavy cream
4 tablespoons grated mature Cheddar cheese
salt and pepper

Rich Shortcrust Pastry:
1 cup all-purpose flour
pinch of salt
4 tablespoons margarine or butter
2 tablespoons vegetable shortening
1 egg yolk
1 tablespoon cold water

couscous-filled
zucchini

4 large zucchini

2 tablespoons lemon juice

I tablespoon olive oil

½ cup mature **Cheddar cheese,** grated

¼ cup **Parmesan cheese,** freshly grated

chopped coriander (cilantro) and coriander (cilantro) sprigs, to garnish

Filling:

3 tablespoons couscous

⅔ cup boiling water

2 tablespoons olive oil

I large onion, minced

3 garlic cloves, minced

I small green pepper, cored, seeded, and diced

I small red chili pepper, seeded and finely chopped

I x 13-ounce can chopped plum tomatoes

⅓ cup black olives, pitted, and sliced

2 tablespoons double concentrate tomato paste

I teaspoon light brown sugar

3 tablespoons finely chopped coriander (cilantro)

salt and pepper

This recipe was a popular dish in my delicatessen and restaurant, and has been a family favorite over the years. I allow I large eggplant per person for a main course, half a small to medium eggplant for a first course. Serve them either hot or cold, with thick natural yogurt flavored with chopped coriander (cilantro) and lime juice, or with Spicy Tomato Sauce (page 232).

1 Cut the zucchini in half lengthwise. With a sharp, pointed knife, draw a shallow line around the flesh about ¼ inch in from the skin. Make criss-cross cuts in the flesh and rub the cut surface with lemon juice. Brush the skin with a little oil. Arrange the zucchini skin-side down on an oiled cookie sheet and place in a preheated 475 degree oven, for about 30 minutes until the flesh is tender.

2 Meanwhile, make the filling. Soak the couscous in the boiling water. Heat the oil and fry the onion and garlic until soft but not colored, then add the pepper and chili pepper and continue to fry until beginning to color. Stir in the tomatoes, olives, tomato paste, sugar, and coriander (cilantro). Cover and cook over a gentle heat for about 20 minutes.

3 Remove the zucchini from the oven. Using a dessert spoon, carefully scoop out the flesh inside the line, taking care not to damage or break the skin. Chop the flesh finely and add to the filling mixture. Fork through the couscous and add to the filling. Season to taste.

4 Pile the filling in the eggplant shells. Mix together the Cheddar and Parmesan cheeses, scatter over the filling and return to the oven for 15–30 minutes until crisp and golden brown. Garnish with chopped coriander (cilantro) and coriander (cilantro) sprigs before serving.

Serves 4

CHEF'S TIP If the filling is very hot when the shells are filled, you can melt the cheese topping under a very hot broiler. The couscous filling is excellent for other vegetables, such as and peppers, and it can also be used in a moussaka instead of meat.

spinach & cheese phyllo pie

8 cups fresh spinach or I pound
   frozen spinach

2 tablespoons olive oil

I large onion, minced

3 garlic cloves, crushed

⅓ cup feta cheese, crumbled

⅓ cup ricotta or cottage cheese

4 tablespoons freshly grated
   Parmesan cheese

2 tablespoons minced parsley

3 eggs, beaten

freshly grated nutmeg

6 tablespoons unsalted butter

12–14 sheets fresh or defrosted phyllo
   pastry, each sheet measuring
   12½ x 7½ inches

pepper

This recipe, with its filling of spinach, cheese and eggs, is based on the Greek phyllo pie known as spanakopitta. *Although feta is the traditional cheese to use, I have used a combination of feta for sharpness and saltiness, ricotta or cottage cheese for a cool mellow taste, and Parmesan, which melts during cooking and holds the filling together.*

1 Remove any large tough spines from the spinach and wash in cold salted water. Shake to remove excess water, then put the spinach into a large saucepan with only the water that clings to the leaves. Cover with foil and a lid and cook over a moderate heat until the spinach is tender, shaking the pan occasionally. This will take 5–8 minutes. Drain well and press out as much water as possible, then chop roughly and put into a large bowl.

2 Heat the oil in a skillet and fry the onion and garlic until soft but not colored. Add to the spinach. Cool, then add the feta, ricotta, or cottage cheese, Parmesan, and parsley. Mash together with a fork. Stir in the beaten eggs and season with nutmeg and pepper. Mix well.

3 Melt the butter and generously butter a shallow 8-inch circular or square cake pan with a removable base or an ovenproof dish 1–1½ inches deep. Use the rest to brush each sheet of phyllo pastry before peeling the sheet off the pile. Work carefully with the pastry, using only one sheet at a time as required. Keep the rest of the phyllo pastry covered with plastic wrap and a damp kitchen towel to prevent it from drying out and becoming brittle.

4 Line the pan with 2–3 sheets of phyllo pastry, pushing it into the sides, and letting the surplus overhang the edges. Butter another 6 sheets, fold each one in half lengthwise and place over the pan, angling them all slightly differently so that the points of the overhanging edges radiate like the petals of a flower. Spoon in the spinach mixture. Lay 2 more sheets of buttered phyllo pastry on top, tucking them in to fit the pie. Bring the overhanging lining sheets over the top layer of pastry, then place the last 3 sheets on top, scrunching them to fit into the pan. Brush the pastry well with butter, then bake in a preheated 375 degree oven, for 45–60 minutes until crisp and golden-brown.

5 Cool slightly, then remove from the pan by inverting a serving plate over the pie and unmolding it. Put another plate over the bottom of the pie and turn it the right way up. Serve hot or cold.

Serves 6–8

broccoli
& coriander chicken

This was one of my mother's favorites, often served for Monday supper — made from the leftovers of Sunday's roast chicken. In this recipe I use raw chicken and gently poach it in chicken broth before combining it with the broccoli. The sauce is lighter and sharper than the original, using crème fraîche rather than a classic béchamel. I have also added curry paste for a touch of spice, but it is equally good without it. Serve with a crisp green salad and garlic bread.

1 Cut the chicken into finger strips, about 3½ x ¾ inches long. Heat the broth, then poach the chicken gently for 4–6 minutes until just cooked. Remove the chicken from the broth with a slotted spoon and set aside.

2 Trim the broccoli into flowerets and peel the stalks. Plunge the flowerets into a large pan of boiling water, cook for 2 minutes, then drain. Refresh under cold running water until very cold. Drain again and dry with paper towels.

3 Prepare the topping by melting the butter in a large skillet and gently frying the bread crumbs until golden brown.

4 Make the sauce. Melt the butter in a large saucepan and fry the onion and garlic until soft but not colored. Stir in the curry paste and fry for a few minutes to develop the flavor. Add the crème fraîche, lemon juice, and coriander (cilantro), season to taste with salt and pepper and mix well. Bring to a boil.

5 Arrange the cooked chicken in a 12 x 9 x 2 inch baking dish. Pour the hot sauce over the chicken. Scatter the cheese on top followed by the bread crumbs. Bake in a preheated 400 degree oven, for 30–40 minutes until bubbling hot and golden brown. To crisp the top, broil under a preheated broiler, if necessary.

Serves 6

**4 boneless, skinless chicken breast
fillets, total weight 1¼–1½ pounds**
2½ cups chicken broth
3 cups broccoli

Gratin Topping:
4 tablespoons butter
1 cup fresh white bread crumbs
**4–6 tablespoons grated mature
Cheddar cheese**

Sauce:
4 tablespoons butter
1 large onion, minced
3 garlic cloves, crushed
2–3 tablespoons curry paste
3 cups crème fraîche
1½ tablespoons lemon juice
**3 tablespoons finely chopped
coriander (cilantro)**
salt and pepper

endive & smoked bacon gratin

Endive has a slightly bitter taste and delicately wilted texture when cooked. It combines beautifully with rich creamy sauces and sharp, piquant flavors like lemon and orange juice, olives, capers, and anchovies. In this recipe I have fried the heads in butter and lemon juice before sprinkling them with crisp bacon. They are then baked in cream flavored with Dijon mustard and cheese. Wicked, but delicious.

1 Trim a thin slice from the root end of the endive, if discolored, and remove any damaged or brown leaves. If it is just the tips of the leaves that have developed a brown edge, trim them with scissors. Cut each endive head in half lengthwise and remove the central core, leaving the head intact.

2 Melt the butter in a large skillet, add the endive cut-side down, and sprinkle with the lemon juice. Fry until browning, turning several times and taking care to keep the heads together.

3 Transfer the endive to a 2–2½ quart gratin dish and scatter with the fried bacon. Mix together the mustard, cream, and two-thirds of the cheese, season with salt and pepper and pour over the endive. Scatter over the remaining cheese and place in a preheated 400–425 degree oven for about 20 minutes until bubbling and golden. Finish the browning under a hot broiler, if necessary. Garnish with chervil sprigs and serve.

Serves 4

8 endive heads
2 tablespoons butter
juice of 1 large lemon
8 large thin slices of lightly smoked bacon, rinded, chopped, and fried until crisp
2 tablespoons Dijon mustard
1¼ cups light cream
⅔ cup grated Swiss or mature Cheddar cheese
salt and pepper
chervil sprigs, to garnish

melange of vegetables
with coconut & cheese topping

In this tasty gratin, the vegetables are fried first, then allowed to cook in their own juices before being moistened with a rich cheese-flavored white sauce and baked in the oven. Serve with brown rice, a crisp salad, and Cucumber & Mint Raita (page 216.)

1 Heat the oil in a large skillet and fry the onion and garlic until soft but not colored. Add the mushrooms and fry until browning. Add the peppers, zucchini, and cauliflower and fry for a few minutes. Add the chili powder, cumin, and turmeric, and season with salt and pepper. Stir well to combine and sauté for a few minutes to develop the flavors. Press a piece of aluminum foil on top of the vegetables and sweat them gently for 20 minutes to draw out the juices, stirring occasionally. The vegetables will produce their own liquid, but if they show signs of drying out and sticking, add a few tablespoons of water.

2 While the vegetables are cooking, prepare the cheese sauce. Melt the butter in a saucepan and stir in the flour. Remove from the heat and gradually blend in the warm milk, making sure no lumps form. Return the pan to the heat and stir constantly until the sauce has thickened. Add the mustard and half of the Cheddar cheese and season to taste with salt and pepper. Stir in the coconut and coriander (cilantro).

3 Pour the sauce over the vegetables and carefully fold in with a large spoon. Tip into a 2 quart gratin dish and scatter the rest of the cheese on top. Bake in a preheated oven at 425 degrees, for 30–40 minutes until bubbling. Alternatively, brown under a preheated broiler. Serve immediately.

Serves 4

3 tablespoons sunflower oil
I large onion, minced
2 garlic cloves, crushed
I½ cups mushrooms, sliced
2 small bell peppers (I red, I green), cored, seeded and cut into ½ inch pieces
2 zucchini, sliced into rings
¼ large cauliflower, broken into flowerets
I teaspoon chili powder
I teaspoon ground cumin
I teaspoon ground turmeric
salt and pepper

Cheese Sauce:
2 tablespoons butter
2 tablespoons all-purpose flour
I¼ cups warm milk
½ teaspoon English mustard powder
⅔–¾ cup grated mature Cheddar cheese
4 tablespoons coconut flakes
3 tablespoons finely chopped coriander (cilantro)
salt and pepper

potato, mushroom, & bacon gratin

2 tablespoons butter

2 tablespoons olive oil

8 slices of lean bacon, rinded and cut
  into strips

I large onion, minced

2 garlic cloves, crushed

⅓ cup mushrooms, sliced

1½–2 pounds cooked potatoes (boiled
  or steamed with their skins on)

⅔–¾ cup heavy cream

I tablespoon minced parsley

6 tablespoons grated Cheddar cheese

4 tablespoons Parmesan cheese,
  freshly grated

salt and pepper

Use a floury potato such as Maris Piper, King Edward, or Pentland Square, which will absorb the cooking juices and make the sauce thick and rich.

1 Melt half of the butter with half of the oil and fry the bacon until browning. Remove from the pan with a slotted spoon and put into a large bowl. Add the remaining butter and oil if necessary and fry the onion and garlic until soft. Add the mushrooms and continue to fry until all the vegetables are beginning to color. With the slotted spoon, transfer all the vegetables to the bowl with the bacon and mix together.

2 Cut the potatoes into wedges and arrange them with the other vegetables in an ovenproof gratin dish. Mix the cream with the parsley, season with salt and pepper and pour it over the vegetables. Mix the Cheddar and Parmesan cheeses together and scatter on top. Set the dish on a cookie sheet and bake in a preheated 350 degree oven, for 20–30 minutes until crisp and golden. Serve immediately.

Serves 4

red lentil, pepper, & mushroom bake

This has been a family favorite for many years. It is rich and substantial, with a deep earthy flavor. As the lentils need to be cooked to a paste, it is best to use the split red variety. They don't need to be presoaked. Other suitable vegetables instead of the pepper and mushrooms are diced zucchini and zucchini, tomatoes and celery, in any combination. Serve with a salad of mixed leaves or crunchy green vegetables.

1 Put the lentils into a saucepan and cover with the boiling water. Return to a boil, then reduce the heat and simmer gently for about 20 minutes, stirring occasionally, until the lentils are tender and all the water has been absorbed.

2 Lightly oil a 1 quart ovenproof dish about 2 inches deep. Heat the rest of the oil in a large pan and fry the onion until soft but not colored. Add the green bell pepper and mushrooms and fry for about 10 minutes on a higher heat to color the vegetables slightly.

3 Add the lentils, chili powder, Tabasco, paprika, tomato paste, tamari sauce, bouillon cube, salt, and pepper. Stir well to combine, then turn into the dish.

4 Mix the topping ingredients together and sprinkle over the lentil mixture. Bake in a preheated 375 degree oven, for about 30 minutes, or until bubbling hot and toasted golden. Serve hot.

Serves 4

¾ cup split red lentils
2½ cups boiling water
3 tablespoons sunflower or olive oil
1 large onion, minced
1 large green bell pepper, cored, seeded and diced
¾ cup mushrooms, sliced
1 teaspoon chili powder
½ teaspoon Tabasco sauce
1 teaspoon paprika
1 tablespoon tomato paste
2 tablespoons tamari sauce
1 bouillon cube
salt and pepper

Topping:
2 tablespoons whole-wheat bread crumbs
2 tablespoons pine nuts, chopped
2 tablespoons pumpkin seeds (pepitas)
4 tablespoons grated Cheddar cheese

dips & salsas

sweet & sour
eggplant relish

This is a tangy relish that is excellent with samosas, Vegetable Beignets (page 130) or Vegetable Pakoras (page 132.) It will keep for about 1 week in the refrigerator.

1 Heat 2 tablespoons of the oil and fry the onion and garlic until soft and beginning to color. Using a slotted spoon, transfer to a large saucepan.

2 Heat one-third of the remaining oil until very hot and fry one-third of the eggplant very quickly until browned on all sides. Using the slotted spoon, transfer them to the pan with the onion. Repeat with the remaining oil and eggplant.

3 Stir the lemon juice, sugar, cumin, and cayenne into the fried eggplant and onion mixture and season with salt to taste. Return to the heat and cover closely with a circle of aluminum foil and the saucepan lid. Cook gently, stirring occasionally, for about 20 minutes until the mixture is thick and pulpy but still with texture.

4 Transfer to a bowl and leave to cool. Cover and refrigerate until required. Serve at room temperature.

Makes 1 quart, enough to serve 8–10

⅓ **cup sunflower oil**

1 large onion, halved and thinly sliced

3 garlic cloves, crushed

2 pounds firm eggplant, cut into
   ½ inch dice

6 tablespoons lemon juice

3–4 tablespoons light brown sugar

1 teaspoon ground cumin

¼ **teaspoon cayenne pepper**

salt

Sweet & Sour Eggplant Relish is shown on page 208

salsa verde

6 tablespoons minced flat leaf parsley

3 tablespoons finely chopped basil

2 garlic cloves, crushed

2 tablespoons capers, drained, rinsed and finely chopped

2 canned anchovy fillets, rinsed and finely chopped

1 teaspoon Dijon mustard

⅓ cup olive oil

1–3 tablespoons lemon juice or white wine vinegar

pepper

This rich, unctuous sauce is perfect with boiled artichokes, grilled vegetables, or steak. It is also delicious tossed with warm pasta, baby new potatoes, cooked navy, Great Northern or pinto beans, or hard-boiled eggs.

1 Combine the parsley, basil, garlic, capers, anchovies, and mustard in a bowl, whisk in the oil and add lemon juice or wine vinegar to sharpen. Transfer to a screw-top jar and store in the refrigerator for up to 1 week.

Makes 1 cup, enough to serve 8

CHEF'S TIP Don't over-chop the ingredients — they should have a little texture rather than being pounded to a pulp. You can add a little variety by using other fresh herbs, such as lovage, fennel fronds, chervil, or arugula, with the parsley, or you can include the finely grated rind from the lemon with the juice. Alternatively, add 1 tablespoon finely chopped pickle instead of the capers and lime or orange juice instead of the lemon.

hot tomato salsa

1 Put the red onion into a small bowl and cover with boiling water. Leave for a few minutes, then drain and refresh under cold water. Drain again and pat dry with paper towels.

2 Combine all the ingredients together, mixing lightly. Cover and chill for 30–60 minutes, to let the flavors develop before serving.

Makes 1¾ cups, enough to serve 4

VARIATIONS Any of the following can be added to the basic tomato salsa: avocado, peeled, diced and tossed in lime juice to prevent discoloration; papaya, peeled, seeded and diced; pineapple, peeled and diced; mango, peeled, stoned and diced; chopped fresh herbs, such as mint, fennel, lovage, oregano, marjoram, dill, tarragon. For a milder salsa, leave out the chili.

1 small red onion, finely diced

1 garlic clove, minced

1 pound sweet ripe tomatoes, peeled, seeded, and diced

1–2 sweet, moderately hot red chili peppers, seeded and finely chopped

3 tablespoons finely chopped coriander (cilantro)

1 tablespoon finely chopped parsley

juice of ½ lime

3 tablespoons olive oil

pinch of salt

pinch of sugar

pepper

Salsa Verde is shown on page 208 and Hot Tomato Salsa is shown on page 209

avocado & tomato salsa

2–3 tablespoons lime juice

1 tablespoon olive oil

a few drops of Tabasco sauce

1 small garlic clove, finely chopped

½ small red onion, finely diced

2 large firm, ripe tomatoes, peeled, seeded, and finely diced

2 large firm, ripe avocados, pitted, peeled, and diced

2 tablespoons finely chopped coriander (cilantro)

salt and pepper

1 Put the lime juice, olive oil, Tabasco and garlic in a bowl and whisk well to combine. Stir in the onion, add the diced tomato and avocado and toss gently in the dressing along with the chopped coriander. Season to taste.

Serves 4

hot papaya & roasted pepper salsa

A sweet, tangy salsa, the color of a flaming sunset, this is warm and inviting to look at and refreshing to eat. Delicious with broiled, grilled, and fried meats, chicken, fish, and vegetables.

1 Combine the lime juice, olive oil, and herb vinegar in a bowl. Add the papayas, chili, spring onions and roasted red peppers and toss gently until combined. Season with salt and pepper and stir in the coriander. Cover and chill for about 30 minutes before serving to allow the flavors to blend and develop. Best eaten on the same day.

Makes 1 pound

juice of 1–2 limes

4 tablespoons light olive oil

¼ teaspoon herb vinegar

2 ripe papayas, halved, seeded and cut into ½ inch dice

½ small red chili pepper, finely chopped

2 green onions (scallions), finely sliced

2 roasted red peppers, cored, seeded and cut into ¼ inch dice

1 tablespoon finely chopped coriander (cilantro)

salt and pepper

charbroiled corn & avocado salsa

This is delicious with broiled or roasted meats and fish, Red Lentil Burgers (page 176), Vegetable Brochettes (page 180) and Grilled Vegetables (page 186). If it is kept longer than a few hours the avocado will discolor and lose its vibrancy, so make it only far enough ahead to allow the flavors to mingle and develop. Alternatively, prepare the salsa in advance without the avocado, adding it about 30 minutes before serving. An excellent variation is to omit the avocado altogether and replace it with another corn-on-the-cob and a small diced red pepper.

1 Plunge the corn cobs into a pan of boiling water, return to a boil and blanch for 3–4 minutes. Drain, rub with a little of the olive oil, and place under a preheated very hot grill for 10–15 minutes until tender and well toasted. Leave to cool slightly, then scrape the kernels from the cobs with a knife; you need about ⅔ cup. Put the kernels into a bowl and set aside to cool.

2 Put the onion in a small bowl and cover with boiling water. Leave for a few minutes, then drain and refresh under cold water. Drain again and pat dry with paper towels. Add the onion to the corn with the lime juice, jalapeño sauce, chili, red pepper, tomato, ground and chopped coriander (cilantro), the remaining oil, and salt, and pepper. Toss gently to combine, then fold in the avocado. Taste and adjust the seasoning as necessary. Cover and refrigerate until required.

Serves 4

2 **corn-on-the-cob, stripped of husks and threads**

3 **tablespoons olive oil**

1 **tablespoon red onion, finely diced**

3–4 **tablespoons lime juice**

2 **dashes of jalapeño sauce**

1 **small red chili, seeded, and finely diced**

¼ **small red pepper, cored, seeded and finely diced**

1 **large firm, red plum tomato, peeled, seeded and finely diced**

¼ **teaspoon ground coriander (cilantro)**

2 **tablespoons finely chopped coriander (cilantro)**

1 **firm, ripe avocado, pitted, peeled, and diced**

salt and pepper

black olive salsa
with capers, onion, & anchovies

This salsa is wonderful to look at and delicious to eat. Serve it on bruschetta, with pasta or seared salmon steaks, or as part of a mixed leaf salad with fresh Parmesan shavings.

1 Drain the anchovy fillets, rinse well under cold running water, and soak in a little milk while preparing the rest of the ingredients.

2 Put the red onion into a small bowl and cover with boiling water. Leave for a few minutes, then drain and refresh under cold water. Drain again and pat dry with paper towels.

3 Remove the anchovies from the milk and rinse well under cold running water. Pat dry with paper towels and chop roughly. Put into a bowl and add the rest of the ingredients. Stir to combine, cover and leave to marinate for at least 30 minutes. The salsa will keep for several days in the refrigerator.

Makes 2 cups, enough to serve 5–6

1 x 2 ounce can anchovy fillets in oil
milk, for soaking
2 tablespoons red onion, finely diced
2 tablespoons red pepper, cored, seeded, and finely diced
2 tablespoons capers in salt or vinegar, drained and rinsed
⅔ cup black olives, pitted and diced
2 large garlic cloves, minced
1 small red chili, seeded and finely chopped
⅔ cup extra virgin olive oil
1 tablespoon lemon juice
1 tablespoon herb vinegar
2 tablespoons finely chopped coriander (cilantro)
3 tablespoons finely chopped flat leaf parsley
pepper

avocado salsa

The word salsa *means sauce, in both Italian and Mexican cooking. In Mexico and the United States it is generally used to describe a slightly chunky relish based on chili peppers, tomatoes, onion, garlic, coriander (cilantro), and salt. There are many variations on this theme, but in general salsas are characterized by their vibrant colors and hand-chopped ingredients. They make a refreshing addition to broiled foods, such as chicken, fish, steaks, lamb cutlets, burgers and patties, sausages, and kabobs, and are equally good piled on top of bruschetta or crostini to be served as a snack or light lunch.*

1 Run a cut line lengthwise through the center of the avocado as far as the pit, then gently twist the two halves apart. The pit will remain in one half. Remove the pit carefully without damaging the delicate flesh. Peel off the skin and cut the avocado into ½ inch dice.

2 Put the avocado flesh into a bowl with the lime juice, coriander (cilantro) and green onions (scallions.) Season to taste with salt and pepper and toss lightly to combine without breaking up the avocado. Cover and refrigerate until required.

Serves 4

1 firm, ripe avocado
2 tablespoons lime juice
1 tablespoon finely chopped
   coriander
2 green onions (scallions), finely sliced
salt and pepper

cucumber & mint raita

A mild-flavored and refreshing Indian yogurt dish, this is the perfect accompaniment to any spicy, highly seasoned meat, fish or vegetable, and traditionally served with Vegetable Pakoras (page 132.) Occasionally I add a little chopped fresh chili pepper or mint sauce, or some freshly chopped coriander (cilantro.)

1 Put the yogurt in a bowl and beat lightly with a fork or whisk until smooth. Add the remaining ingredients and stir to combine. Cover and refrigerate until required. Serve chilled, garnished with mint sprigs.

Makes 1¼ cups, enough to serve 4–6

1 cup plain yogurt
3-inch piece of cucumber, peeled and
    coarsely grated or chopped
2 tablespoons chopped mint
pinch of ground cumin
pepper
squeeze of lemon or lime juice
mint sprigs, to garnish

mango & cucumber
salsa with chili

This salsa is quick and easy to make, and can be as fiery or cooling as you wish — simply adjust the amount of chili peppers or leave them out altogether. It is excellent with broiled, roasted, or fried foods, particularly whitefish and salmon, but is also perfect with cold meats, such as salami, bresaola, or country ham. It will keep for several days in the refrigerator.

½ cucumber, peeled

1 large mango, ripe but still
  firm

3 tablespoons minced
  red onion

1 small green chili, seeded and
  finely chopped

1 tablespoon minced flat leaf
  parsley

juice of 1½ limes

salt and pepper

minced flat leaf parsley, to garnish

1 Cut the cucumber into ⅛–¼ inch cubes and leave in a sieve to drain. Cut down each side of the flat central pit of the mango. Discard the pit and cut each piece of mango flesh into long strips ⅛–¼ inch thick. Remove the skin by slipping the knife between the flesh and skin and running it along its length. Cut into dice. Combine the cucumber and mango in a bowl.

2 Put the onion in a small bowl, cover with boiling water, and soak for a few minutes. Drain and refresh under cold water, then pat dry with paper towels (this helps to soften the flavor of the onion.)

3 Add the onion to the cucumber and mango with the rest of the ingredients. Stir gently to combine. Cover and chill for a few hours to allow the flavors to mingle and develop. Serve chilled, garnished with minced flat leaf parsley.

Makes 2½ cups, enough to serve 6

guacamole

This thick creamy purée from Mexico can be used as a dip for Raw Vegetable Platter (page 129,) fresh tortilla chips or hot pita bread, or eaten Mexican-style with tortillas. It can also be used as a sauce for fish and chicken. Don't purée the avocado flesh in a food processor or blender as this produces too smooth a texture.

1 Put the avocado flesh in a bowl along with the lime or lemon juice and mash with a fork to make a textured paste. Stir in the garlic, onion, tomato, chili peppers, coriander (cilantro), and sugar. Season with salt and pepper and add some extra lime or lemon juice, if required. Spoon the mixture into a serving bowl and garnish with coriander (cilantro) sprigs. Cover with plastic wrap to prevent discoloration and chill in the refrigerator until required.

Makes about 2 cups

2 large ripe avocados, halved, pitted, and peeled
juice of 1 lime or lemon
1 garlic clove, crushed
1 tablespoon finely chopped onion
1 large tomato, skinned, seeded and finely diced
1–2 fresh green chili peppers, seeded. and finely chopped
1 tablespoon finely chopped coriander (cilantro)
pinch of sugar
salt and pepper
coriander (cilantro) sprigs, to garnish

lentil, green peppercorn,
& mustard dip

Serve with crisp vegetables or fried or grilled fish. It also goes well with Raw Vegetable Platter (page 129), Vegetable Brochettes (page 180), or Broiled Vegetables (page 186.)

1 Bring a large saucepan of water to a boil, add the lentils, and return to a boil. Cook for 10–15 minutes until just tender and beginning to turn mushy. Drain and refresh under cold water until completely cold.
2 Crush the peppercorns until roughly broken, using a pestle and mortar. Stir in the mustard and beat in the oil, adding a little at a time. Stir in the lemon juice, warm water, and cooked lentils. Pile into a serving bowl, cover with plastic wrap, and store in the refrigerator. The dip will keep for several days.

Makes ⅔ cup

2 tablespoons green Puy lentils
1–2 tablespoons green peppercorns in brine, drained
2 tablespoons Dijon mustard
4 tablespoons sunflower oil
1 tablespoon lemon juice
1 tablespoon warm water

harissa

This is a traditional North African accompaniment to soups, stews, and couscous. It is fiery hot and not for the faint-hearted. Some more aromatic versions include herbs like mint and coriander (cilantro), but they are no less fiery. Harissa can be bought in tubes and cans from Middle Eastern food stores and gourmet stores. The only substitute is a spicy paste from Indonesia called sambal oelek. *A simple version of harissa can be made quickly by adding as much Tabasco sauce, paprika, cayenne pepper, and crushed garlic as you like to tomato purée along with a little oil and lemon juice.*

1 If using dried chili peppers, soak them with or without their seeds in hot water for 1 hour. The seeds add to the fiery taste of the harissa.

2 Wearing rubber gloves, drain the chili peppers and cut them into small pieces. If using fresh chili peppers, seed them if desired, then chop finely. Pound in a mortar with the garlic and salt until puréed, or blend in a food processor or blender. I find pounding more successful as it gives a finer purée.

3 Put the coriander, cumin, and caraway seeds in a dry skillet and shake over a low heat for a few minutes to roast and develop their flavor. Grind in a spice mill and add to the chili mixture with enough oil to make a thick paste. Blend again. Put into a screw-top jar and drizzle on enough oil to cover and seal. Cover with a lid and store in the refrigerator until required. It will keep for several months.

Makes ⅓ cup

50 g (2 oz) dried or fresh red chili peppers
4 garlic cloves, crushed
½ tablespoon salt
½–1 teaspoon coriander (cilantro) seeds
½–1 teaspoon cumin seeds
½–1 teaspoon caraway seeds
1–2 tablespoons sunflower oil

chili bean dip

This spicy dip is excellent with raw vegetables, corn chips, or fingers of warmed or toasted pita bread. It is also good spread on bruschetta and crostini, like a pâté.

1 Halve the peppers lengthwise and deseed. Lightly brush the pepper inside and out with a little oil. Place on a lightly oiled cookie sheet and roast in a pre-heated 475 degree oven for 15 minutes. Turn the peppers over and continue to roast until the edges begin to blacken and the flesh and skin begin to crumple. This will probably take another 15 minutes. Remove the peppers from the oven and leave until cool enough, then peel off the skins.

2 Grind the red pepper flesh, garlic, and chili in a food processor or blender until well chopped. Add the beans and paprika and continue to process until a coarse purée forms. This won't take long. Season with Tabasco (if using) and salt and pepper. With the machine running, add the rest of the oil to make a thick paste.

3 Pile the bean purée into a bowl and sprinkle with the chives. Cover and refrigerate until required.

Makes about ¾ cup, enough to serve 4

2 large red peppers

2 tablespoons olive oil

2 garlic cloves, crushed

1 small red chili, seeded and finely chopped

1 x 13 ounce can red kidney beans, drained

½ teaspoon paprika

few drops of Tabasco sauce (if required)

salt and pepper

2 tablespoons snipped chives, to garnish

eggplant & sesame dip

1½ pounds eggplant

3 tablespoons lemon juice

2 tablespoons olive oil

2 garlic cloves, crushed

5 tablespoons finely chopped
  coriander (cilantro) or flat leaf
  parsley

3 tablespoons tahini paste

dash of Tabasco sauce

½ tablespoon white sugar

¼ teaspoon chili powder

2 tablespoons thick plain yogurt

salt and pepper

To Serve:

coriander (cilantro) or flat leaf
  parsley sprigs

paprika or black pepper

1 tablespoon toasted sesame seeds

This smooth and smoky-tasting paste makes an excellent dip for raw vegetables or warm pita bread. It can also be used as a spread for crostini, bruschetta, or crackers. In a covered bowl, it keeps for about 1 week in the refrigerator.

1 Cut the eggplant in half lengthwise and brush the cut sides with lemon juice. Brush a heavy baking sheet with a little olive oil, place the eggplant cut-side downward on the sheet, and bake in a preheated 475 degree oven for 20–30 minutes until the flesh is tender and the shells collapsed. Turn them cut-side up and leave to cool.

2 With a metal spoon, scoop the eggplant flesh into a food processor or blender. Add the garlic, coriander (cilantro), or parsley and the remaining lemon juice and blender to form a smooth purée. Add the tahini, Tabasco, sugar, chili powder, yogurt, and salt and pepper to taste, and blend again. Taste for seasoning.

3 Pile the dip into a bowl and float the remaining oil on top. Cover and chill until required. Before serving, stir in the oil and garnish with coriander (cilantro) or parsley sprigs, a little paprika or black pepper and the toasted sesame seeds.

Makes about 2½ cups, enough to serve 5

hummus

1 x 13 ounce can chickpeas (garbanzo
    beans) or ⅓ cup dried chickpeas
    (garbanzo beans), soaked and
    cooked
2 garlic cloves, crushed
2–3 tablespoons lemon juice
⅓ cup tahini paste
about ⅓ cup olive or
    sunflower oil
2–4 tablespoons natural set yogurt,
    chickpea cooking liquid or hot water
salt and pepper
cayenne or paprika pepper, to serve

It takes seconds to make hummus using canned chickpeas and a food processor or blender, and it is much less expensive and much tastier than buying it ready made.

1 Drain and rinse the chickpeas (reserving the cooking liquor if you are using dried chickpeas) and put them into a food processor or blender with the garlic, lemon juice, tahini paste, 1 teaspoon salt, and pepper to taste. Process to a smooth paste.

2 Very gradually add the oil as if you were making mayonnaise. Stir in the yogurt, cooking liquor, or hot water to give the required consistency. Taste and adjust the seasoning, if necessary.

3 Spoon the hummus into a serving dish and smooth with the back of a spoon. Pour over a little oil and dust with a sprinkling of cayenne or paprika.

Makes 1¼–1½ cups, enough to serve 4

skordalia

This garlicky purée is the Greek equivalent of Aïoli (opposite page). It was traditionally served with fried vegetables during Lent, as it was made without egg. Breadcrumbs, mashed potatoes, ground almonds or walnuts were used instead.

1 Crush the garlic and pound with the salt using a pestle and mortar (or use a heavy bowl and the end of a wooden rolling pin). Soak the bread in the hot water until it forms a thick paste. Add to the garlic and pound well to blend. Continue to pound while gradually adding the almonds.

2 When the mixture is a homogenous mass, start adding the oil very gradually, drop by drop at first, just like making mayonnaise. Pound well between each addition until the sauce is thick, rich and emulsified. Add lemon juice to taste, pepper and extra salt if required. If the sauce is too thick, add more oil and a little hot water to give the desired consistency.

Makes 1¾ cups, enough to serve 8–12

1 large head garlic, about 8–10 fat
    cloves, peeled
1 teaspoon salt
2 slices stale white bread, crusts
    removed
5 tablespoons hot water
2 tablespoons ground almonds
½–¾ cup olive oil
2-4 tablespoons lemon juice
freshly ground white pepper

aïoli

This Provençal sauce is a strongly flavored mayonnaise in which garlic is pounded to a very smooth paste before the egg yolks and oil are added. It is not just a case of adding crushed garlic to mayonnaise. The quantity of garlic can range from 4 cloves to 2 heads, depending on taste. It is generally left raw, but whole heads may be roasted first, for a less harsh flavor. Lemon juice may be added to cut through the oil and sharpen the taste, and finely chopped herbs, such as oregano and flat leaf parsley, can be stirred into the finished sauce for variety. For additional flavor and color, a pinch of saffron can be soaked in 1 tablespoon warm water and added in place of the boiled water. For a less rich sauce, replace half of the olive oil with sunflower oil. Aïoli is traditionally served with salt cod, squid, octopus, lobster, snails, and boiled potatoes.

6 large garlic cloves

2 egg yolks

1¼ cups extra-virgin olive oil

2 tablespoons lemon juice

1 teaspoon cooled boiled water

salt and white pepper

1 Crush the garlic to a smooth paste using a pestle and mortar (or use a heavy bowl and the end of a wooden rolling pin). I generally crush the cloves in a garlic press first.

2 Unless the mortar is very large, transfer the garlic to a large bowl, add the egg yolks, and continue to pound with the pestle, or use an electric hand-mixer. Although the mixer would be frowned on by the purists, it is much quicker and easier. The traditional method is time-consuming, and food processors or blenders are unsuitable because they make the garlic bitter.

3 When the garlic and yolks are well blended, begin adding the oil, just as when making mayonnaise, drop by drop to begin with, until the sauce begins to thicken and about half of the oil has been added. Continue to add the oil in a thin stream, beating all the time. If the mayonnaise becomes too thick, add a few drops of the lemon juice. Continue like this until all the oil and lemon juice have been incorporated. The consistency should be very thick, almost solid, and rich and glistening. Season with salt and pepper and stabilize with the cooled boiled water. If the sauce should curdle or separate (because the oil has been added too quickly and the mixture not beaten well enough), put a third egg yolk into a fresh bowl and very gradually beat the curdled aïoli into it until it holds again.

4 Pile the sauce into a bowl, cover, and store in the refrigerator until required. The garlic flavor will continue to develop for several hours after the sauce has been made.

Makes about 1¼ cups, enough to serve 4

Indonesian peanut dipping sauce

This recipe was inspired by one of my favorite sauces, satay, the rich, spicy, nutty Indonesian concoction made from peanuts, peanut butter, ginger, and chili powder. In this recipe I have made the sauce thicker and richer than normal so that it can be used as a dip. It is delicious with any type of vegetable brochette or kabob, with chunky pieces of broiled vegetables and broiled skewered meats, particularly chicken.

1 Heat the oil in a saucepan and fry the onion, garlic, ginger, and ground peanuts for 10 minutes to develop the flavors. Add the rest of the ingredients, stirring well to combine. Bring to a boil, reduce the heat and cook gently for a further 10 minutes. The sauce will be thick and rich.

Makes 1 cup

2 tablespoons sunflower oil

I small onion, finely grated

2 garlic cloves, crushed

I inch piece of fresh root ginger, peeled and grated

2 tablespoons dry roasted peanuts, ground in a blender or nut mill

a large pinch of hot chili powder

½ teaspoon soy sauce

2 tablespoons crunchy peanut butter

I–2 tablespoons dark brown sugar

2 tablespoons lime juice

I cup coconut cream

hoisin sauce

A strongly flavored, distinctive, and versatile Chinese sauce, which can be used as a dressing or dip for raw or cooked vegetables. It makes an excellent addition to a stir-fry of leafy greens or robust vegetables, and is a good marinade for meat or fish.

1 Heat the oil and fry the onion, garlic, and ginger until soft but not colored. Add the lemongrass and gradually stir in the rest of the ingredients. Transfer to a bowl or jar, leave to cool, then cover and store in the refrigerator until required. The sauce will keep for several days.

Makes 1¼ cups

3 tablespoons light sesame oil

¼ small onion, minced

2 garlic cloves, minced

I inch piece of fresh root ginger, peeled and finely sliced

I lemongrass stalk, finely chopped

⅓ cup concentrated vegetable broth

5 tablespoons hoisin sauce

2 tablespoons soy sauce

3 tablespoons red wine vinegar

2 tablespoons clear honey

Szechuan dipping sauce

3 tablespoons soy sauce

2 tablespoons light sesame oil

2 tablespoons lime juice

I tablespoon rice wine vinegar

I tablespoon sweet chili sauce

I tablespoon clear honey

2 garlic cloves, finely chopped

I teaspoon toasted sesame seeds

**I inch piece of fresh root ginger,
peeled and finely grated**

**2 large green onions (scallions), finely
chopped**

**I tablespoon finely chopped
coriander (cilantro)**

A hot peppery dipping sauce, which takes its name from the fiery cooking of the Szechuan province of China. Although hot, it is also slightly sweet and spicy. Serve with Raw Vegetable Platter (page 129) and well-flavored broiled vegetables.

1   Combine all the ingredients except the green onions (scallions) and coriander (cilantro) in a screw-top jar. Shake well to combine. Leave for a few hours so that the flavors can mingle and develop.

2   Just before serving, stir in the green onions (scallions) and coriander (cilantro.) This sauce will keep for several weeks, as long as the onions and herbs have not been added.

Makes ⅓ cup.

tapenade

A rich robust purée of olives from Provence. There is no absolute recipe — although most have capers, they are not obligatory; others also include anchovies. Black or green olives can be used. Serve as a dip for Raw Vegetable Platter (page 129), a filling for hard-boiled eggs, or a spread on biscuits, crackers, or crostini. Tapenade can also be tossed with pasta and strongly-flavored vegetables like broccoli, or combined with vinaigrette to be used as a dressing for salads and cold meats.

I cup pitted black olives

**I x 2 ounce can anchovy fillets,
drained and rinsed**

2–3 tablespoons capers, drained

juice of I small lemon

1–2 garlic cloves, crushed

½ teaspoon Dijon mustard

¼ cup extra-virgin olive oil

pepper

1   Put the olives, anchovies, capers, lemon juice, garlic, and mustard into a food processor or blender. With the machine at full speed, pour in the olive oil to produce a coarse or smooth paste as required. Taste and season with pepper, if necessary. Transfer to a screw-top jar and pour a little oil on top to cover and seal. Cover with the lid and refrigerate. It will keep almost indefinitely.

Makes 1 cup

sauces
& dressings

sweet & sour sauce

A hot, spicy sauce to serve with lightly steamed or broiled vegetables, or Vegetable Beignets (page 130), sturdy salad leaves, and broiled meats, poultry, or fish. If stored in an airtight container without the coriander (cilantro) and green onions (scallions), it will keep in the refrigerator for several weeks.

¾ **cup rice wine vinegar**

⅓ **cup water**

2 tablespoons teriyaki sauce

2 tablespoons lime juice

2 tablespoons turbinado sugar

2–3 garlic cloves, crushed

1–3 tablespoons sweet chili sauce

1 tablespoon finely chopped coriander (cilantro)

3 green onions (scallions), minced

salt

1 Combine all the ingredients, except the coriander (cilantro) and spring onions (scallions), in a saucepan. The amount of sweet chili sauce you add will depend on how hot you want the sauce to be and the strength of the sauce itself. Gently bring to a boil, stirring to blend and dissolve the sugar. Reduce the heat and simmer for about 5 minutes. Set aside to cool, then stir in the chopped coriander (cilantro) and green onions (scallions).

Makes 1¼ cups, enough to serve 10–20

Sweet & Sour Sauce is shown on page 226

ginger & lime pickle mayonnaise

This recipe was inspired by the wonderful range of pickles and chutneys made by Mrs Bassa's Indian Kitchen. They're superb just as they are, but mixed with a rich mayonnaise or thick plain yogurt, they make an excellent dip.

1 Using a vegetable peeler, remove the rind from the lime in very thin strips, leaving the white part attached to the flesh. Cut the rind into julienne strips. Remove the white part from the lime with a serrated knife and cut the flesh into segments.

2 Make the mayonnaise. Put the egg yolk and mustard in a bowl, then add the oil, drop by drop, beating continually with a hand or electric whisk. After about 2 tablespoons oil has been incorporated, add the rest in a fine, thread-like stream, still beating continually.

3 Squeeze the juice from half of the lime segments into the mayonnaise, then stir in the remaining lime segments and half of the lime julienne, the pickle or chutney, ginger, and coriander (cilantro.) Season as necessary, garnish with the remaining lime julienne, then cover and refrigerate until required.

Makes 1¼ cups

I lime
I large egg yolk
¼ teaspoon English mustard powder
⅓ cup sunflower oil
4 tablespoons lime pickle, brinjal pickle or mango chutney
I piece stem ginger preserved in syrup, cut into slivers
I tablespoon finely chopped coriander (cilantro)
salt and pepper

Ginger & Lime Pickle Mayonnaise is shown on page 227

fresh basil dressing

1 Put all the ingredients in a screw-top jar and shake vigorously to emulsify.

Makes about 1 cup

⅓ cup extra virgin olive oil

juice of 1 large lemon

4 tablespoons basil leaves, finely
  chopped

pinch of salt

pinch of cracked black peppercorns

vinaigrette

1 Put all the ingredients in a screw-top jar and shake vigorously to emulsify. Taste and adjust the seasoning if necessary.

Makes 6 tablespoons

½ teaspoon Dijon mustard

1 small garlic clove, crushed

2 tablespoons walnut or hazelnut oil

2 tablespoons sunflower oil

1 teaspoon cider or white wine vinegar

salt and pepper

lime & sesame dressing

1 Put all the ingredients in a screw-top jar and shake vigorously to emulsify.

Makes ⅓ cup

4 tablespoons light sesame oil

2 tablespoons sunflower oil

2 tablespoons lime juice

pinch of sugar

salt and pepper

spicy tomato sauce

A rich, pulpy homemade tomato sauce is one of the essentials in any kitchen. It can be made in large or small quantities, and freezes well, ready for use when needed. In the absence of large, sweet, flavorful, sun-ripened tomatoes, a more satisfactory result is obtained by using canned tomatoes. Shop around, try a few different brands, then stick to the one that gives you the best results. All sorts of flavors can be added to the basic sauce: diced red or green hot chili peppers (seeds removed), Tabasco sauce, olives, anchovy fillets, or fresh herbs like basil and oregano.

1 Heat the oil in a heavy saucepan and fry the onion and garlic until soft but not colored. This will take about 10 minutes. Add the rest of the ingredients. Bring to a boil, then reduce the heat, cover, and simmer for 20 minutes to reduce the liquid and concentrate the flavors. Taste and adjust the seasoning and serve the sauce just as it is, thick and pulpy, or blend to give a smooth finish. It may be necessary to adjust the consistency slightly, depending on how the sauce is to be used.

Makes 2½ cups, enough to serve 4

I tablespoon olive oil
I large onion, minced
2 garlic cloves, finely crushed
I x 13 ounce can chopped plum
  tomatoes
5 tablespoons vegetable broth
2 tablespoons tomato paste
I teaspoon sugar
I bay leaf
I teaspoon finely chopped basil
pinch of ground cinnamon
salt and pepper

Hollandaise sauce

It is a long time since I made Hollandaise sauce the classic way. This food processor method is quick, easy and more or less foolproof.

1 Put the shallot, cracked peppercorns, lemon juice, and vinegar into a small saucepan. Bring to a boil and cook quickly to reduce the liquid to about 2 tablespoons. Strain into a food processor. Add the egg yolks and process for a few seconds to mix.

2 Melt the butter in a small saucepan over a low heat. With the processor motor running, very gradually pour the butter through the funnel in a thin steady stream, leaving the residue from the butter still in the pan. The mixture will thicken very slightly.

3 Pour the sauce into a bowl and set over a pan of simmering water. The water should not touch the bottom of the bowl. Whisk continually with a balloon whisk until the sauce warms and thickens, taking care that it does not overheat or it may separate and curdle. If it begins to show signs of curdling, quickly remove the bowl from the hot water and beat in 1 tablespoon cold water. Season with salt and extra lemon juice or vinegar, if necessary. If you are not serving the sauce immediately, turn the heat down very low and keep the sauce warm, whisking from time to time.

Makes about 1¼ cups, enough to serve 4

l shallot, minced

l teaspoon cracked white peppercorns

4 tablespoons lemon juice

l tablespoon white wine vinegar

3 egg yolks

l cup unsalted butter

sea salt

pesto

The word pesto comes from the Italian word pestare, *meaning "to pound" or "to bruise." The sauce originated in Liguria in northern Italy, and in Provence in the south of France, they make a similar sauce called* pistou. *The ingredients for pesto are traditionally pounded together in a mortar to form a brilliant green paste, slightly speckled in appearance, with a heady perfume and a rich flavor. Today, purists still use a pestle and mortar, but most of us are satisfied with using a food processor or blender. The secret is not to over-process. Pesto can also be made with herbs like parsley, coriander, sage, sorrel, or arugula but with different results. Although traditionally served with pasta, it has many other uses. It can be stirred into risotto or mashed potatoes, or soups such as minestrone, mixed vegetable, and tomato. It can liven up baked tomatoes, sandwiches and crostini, and it combines beautifully with slices of sweet fragrant tomato and buffalo mozzarella cheese.*

1 Put the pine nuts and garlic into a food processor and process briefly. The pesto should not be totally smooth, but have a slight texture. Add the Parmesan and basil and process briefly.

2 With the motor running, gradually add the oil through the funnel in a thin stream until it is all incorporated and a thick, slightly runny paste has formed. Check the seasoning, adding salt and pepper as necessary.

3 Serve as required or store in the refrigerator in an airtight container, covered with a little oil to retain the color. It will keep well for at least 1 month. Once the container is opened, the sauce needs to be used within 2–3 days.

Makes about 1 cup

3 tablespoons pine nuts
3 cloves garlic
1–3 tablespoons freshly grated Parmesan cheese
4 tablespoons basil leaves
⅓ cup light extra virgin olive oil
salt and pepper

mushroom sauce

This richly flavored sauce can be made with cultivated or wild mushrooms, or even a combination of both. It can also be made without the cream. The liquid can be half-broth and half-red wine, or all milk, depending on the result required and what it is to be served with. It is particularly good with savory roulades or pasta.

2 tablespoons butter

1 onion, minced

1 garlic clove, crushed

¼ cup mushrooms, thinly sliced

3 tablespoons butter

3 tablespoons all-purpose flour

2 cups mushroom or
vegetable broth

6 tablespoons cream

salt and pepper

1 Melt the butter in a large saucepan and gently fry the onion over a low heat until soft but not colored. Add the garlic and mushrooms to the saucepan and fry until beginning to color.

2 Melt the butter in another saucepan, stir in the flour and cook for a few minutes. Gradually add the broth, stirring to form a smooth consistency. Bring to a boil, stirring frequently, then cook over a gentle heat for 5 minutes to develop the flavor.

3 Add the cream, and season to taste. Return to a boil and use as required.

Makes 3 cups, enough to serve 8

acco

paniments

seeded cheese crackers

Serve these crisp savory crackers with soup, raw vegetable salads, such as Vegetable Carpaccio (page 128) or Raw Vegetable Platter (page 129), and roasted or broiled vegetables. They are perfect with cheese and chutney too, and also good as a cocktail cracker. They can be cut into any shape, served hot or cold, and they freeze well.

1 cup all-purpose flour

6 tablespoons unsalted butter, cut into small pieces

1 tablespoon English mustard powder

pinch of cayenne pepper

pinch of salt

½ cup finely grated mature Cheddar cheese

3–4 tablespoons finely grated Parmesan cheese

2 tablespoons black mustard seeds

1 tablespoon poppyseeds

1 Work the flour, butter, mustard, cayenne, and salt in a food processor until the mixture resembles fine bread crumbs. Add the Cheddar and continue to process for a few seconds until the mixture begins to come together to make a soft dough. Turn on to a lightly floured surface and knead gently. Wrap in plastic wrap and refrigerate for about 30 minutes.

2 Roll out the pastry on a lightly floured surface to about ⅛ inch thick. Cut into circles with a 2½ inch fluted cookie cutter. Knead the trimmings together, roll out and cut more circles.

3 Line 2 heavy cookie sheets with nonstick baking parchment and place the crackers on them. Sprinkle with Parmesan and dust with mustard and poppy seeds. Bake in a preheated 400 degree oven for 9–12 minutes until crisp and light golden. Transfer to a wire rack with a metal spatula. Serve hot, or set aside to cool and store in an airtight container to serve later.

Makes about 30

Seeded Cheese Crackers are shown on the preceding page

tomato & olive bruschetta

Bruschetta are pieces of coarse-textured crusty country bread, more than two days old, cut into ½ inch slices and toasted on both sides on a ridged cast iron grill pan or barbecue grill. Traditionally they were cooked over a wood fire, but nowadays they are more often grilled or baked in a very hot oven at 425 degrees for about 10 minutes until crisp and golden. While still warm, the toasted bread is rubbed with cut garlic, seasoned with sea salt, and drizzled with fragrant extra-virgin olive oil. Sometimes the bread is brushed with oil before broiling or baking, but this is not strictly authentic. Bruschetta are an excellent way of using up bread which is past its best but not yet stale. It can be served plain, or as a base for an infinite variety of toppings, such as salsa, tapenade, pesto, roasted Mediterranean vegetables, pâté, grilled goats' cheese, sautéed mushrooms, and scrambled eggs.

2 large garlic cloves, peeled

8–10 baby tomatoes, cut into thin slices

8 black olives, pitted and roughly chopped

8 green olives, pitted and roughly chopped

2 sun-dried tomatoes in oil, drained and roughly chopped

3 tablespoons extra virgin olive oil

1 teaspoon balsamic vinegar

2 tablespoons finely chopped flat-leaved parsley

4 slices of bread

4–8 basil leaves, torn into pieces

salt and pepper

1 Finely chop 1 garlic clove and put it in a bowl with the tomatoes, black and green olives, sun-dried tomatoes, half of the oil, and the vinegar. Season with salt and pepper to taste and add half of the parsley. Toss very gently to combine and leave to marinate for 10–15 minutes.

2 Toast the bread on both sides. Cut the remaining garlic clove in half, then lightly rub each side of the toast with the cut sides of the garlic. Brush with the remaining oil. Arrange the bread on a serving plate and spoon the tomato and olive mixture on top. Sprinkle with the remaining parsley and the basil leaves, then drizzle with a little of the remaining oil. Serve immediately.

Makes 4

cheese-flavored leek & herb scones

Scones are a type of biscuit, excellent with savory dishes like soups and stews, and the flavorings can be changed to complement the dish they accompany. Onion or garlic can be used instead of the leek or chives; thyme instead of the basil or marjoram; chili powder, paprika or cayenne instead of black pepper. Finely chopped and fried bacon also gives a very tasty result. If buttermilk is not available, use thin yogurt or sour cream.

1 Sift the flour, double-acting baking powder, and salt into a bowl. Cut the butter into small pieces and rub into the flour until the mixture resembles fine bread crumbs. Stir in half of the Cheddar, the leek or chives, parsley, basil, or marjoram and pepper.

2 Make a well in the center and add almost all of the buttermilk, mixing with a wooden spoon or broad-bladed knife to form a soft dough. Take care not to overwork the dough or it will be heavy and tough. Turn on to a lightly floured surface and knead very gently to form a round shape. Pat or roll the dough to about ¾–1 inch thick, then cut into scones using a 1¾ inch cookie cutter.

3 Place the scones a few inches apart on a lightly floured baking sheet and brush with a little egg or milk to glaze. Top with the remaining cheese and a light dusting of paprika. Bake the scones in a preheated 425 degree oven for 15–20 minutes until risen and golden in color. Serve hot or cold, with butter.

Makes 15

2 cups all-purpose flour, plus extra for dusting
2 teaspoons double-acting baking powder
pinch of salt
2 tablespoons butter, plus extra to serve
4–6 cups grated Cheddar cheese
2 tablespoons finely chopped leek or snipped chives
1 tablespoon minced parsley
1 teaspoon minced basil or marjoram
pinch of black pepper
1 cup buttermilk
beaten egg or milk, to glaze
paprika, for dusting

herbed grain bread

The perfect accompaniment to soups, stews and savory dishes as well as cheese, this bread has a close, coarse texture and nutty flavor. Any flour or combination of flours can be used to create different tastes and textures, and other flavorings can be added, such as finely chopped fried bacon, nuts and seeds, even a strongly flavored grated cheese. For a sweet bread, substitute sugar and dried fruit for the herbs.

1 Thickly spread half of the butter over the inside of a 1 pound loaf pan.

2 Combine the flours, raw oatmeal, sugar, salt and pepper in a large bowl. Sift in the baking soda and cream of tartar and stir to mix well. Cut the remaining butter into small pieces and rub into the mixture until it resembles fine bread crumbs. Add the leek and herbs and mix well to combine.

3 Make a well in the center of the mixture and pour in all but 2 tablespoons of the buttermilk. The quantity of liquid required will depend on the type and absorbency of the flours used. Working quickly and lightly with your hand, mix the buttermilk into the dry ingredients. The less you work the mixture the lighter the bread will be. The mixture should resemble thick, slightly sloppy cooked oatmeal.

4 Scrape the dough into the buttered pan and shape it with a spoon so that it is slightly domed in the center but without any air bubbles. The bread will rise and level out during cooking. Sprinkle with the seeds and a little extra whole-wheat flour, then gently rough up the surface with the prongs of a fork.

5 Cook in a preheated 400 degree oven for 30 minutes, then cover loosely with aluminum foil, reduce the temperature to 350 degrees, and cook for a further 30 minutes.

6 Remove the bread from the oven and leave to cool in the pan, still covered with the foil. When cold, remove from the pan and wrap in a clean kitchen towel or napkin. The bread will keep well for several days and can be reheated in the oven if cut into slices and wrapped in foil.

Makes one 1 pound loaf

4 tablespoons butter
1¼ cups extra-coarse whole-wheat flour
1¼ cups malted grain flour
¾ cup all-purpose flour
¾ cup raw oatmeal
2 tablespoons light brown sugar
1 teaspoon salt
1 tablespoon pepper
2 teaspoons baking soda
1 teaspoon cream of tartar
2 tablespoons finely chopped leek
4 tablespoons minced parsley
2 tablespoons finely snipped chives
1 teaspoon minced thyme
1 teaspoon finely chopped oregano
1¾–2 cups buttermilk
1 tablespoon pumpkin seeds (pepitas), sesame seeds, or poppyseeds

cheese-flavored crisps

These can be served as a savory bite with drinks, or as an accompaniment to soup, roasted vegetables, or leafy salads. The cheese can be mixed with 2 tablespoons chopped walnuts, pecans, or hazelnuts, and seasoned with fresh thyme, ground black pepper, a little paprika, or cayenne. When cold, the crisps can be stored in an airtight container for about 1 week or frozen for several weeks. If they soften, return them to a hot oven to crisp up.

½ cup Cheddar, Swiss, or Jack cheese, coarsely grated or diced

1 Line several baking sheets with nonstick baking paper. Place 2 mounds of cheese on each sheet, no more than 3½ inches in diameter and at least 4 inches apart. The cheese will spread and form rough cookie shapes.

2 Bake in a preheated 425 degree oven for 10 minutes until the cheese bubbles and begins to turn a very pale cream color. If the color is allowed to get any deeper, the cheese will taste bitter.

3 Allow the crisps to cool slightly, then transfer them with a spatula to a wire rack to cool completely. Serve or store as required.

Serves 7–8

Swiss crisps
with pecans & thyme

⅔ cup **Swiss cheese,**
   coarsely grated

2 tablespoons **pecan nuts, walnuts,**
   hazelnuts, or pine nuts, chopped

2 teaspoons **chopped thyme**

pepper

1 teaspoon **hot paprika**

These are perfect with salads, roasted or broiled vegetables, spicy stews and stir-fries. They also make excellent cocktail crackers. They will keep for about 1 week in an airtight container, and can be very quickly crisped up in the oven if they become soft during storage. They can also be frozen in a rigid airtight container.

1 Line a large cookie sheet with nonstick baking paper. Pile small spoonfuls of the grated cheese on the paper, leaving about 4 inches between each pile to allow the cheese to spread. Sprinkle with the nuts and thyme and dust each mound with freshly ground black pepper and a sprinkle of paprika.

2 Bake in a preheated 350 degree oven for 8–12 minutes until the cheese starts to bubble and turn a light golden brown. Take care not to let the cheese brown too much or the crisps will taste bitter.

3 Remove from the oven and allow to cool slightly before transferring to a wire rack with a metal spatula. Leave to cool completely before serving, or store as required.

Makes 14

phyllo & Swiss wafers

These crisp savory wafers are composed of gossamer thin sheets of phyllo pastry layered with butter and finely grated Swiss cheese. Serve with soup, roasted vegetables, salads, and spicy vegetable stir-fries. They make excellent crackers to serve with drinks, and can be stored in an airtight container for 3–4 days.

1 Lightly brush 1 sheet of phyllo pastry with butter and scatter with a little of the cheese. Put a second sheet on top, brush with melted butter and scatter with more cheese. Repeat with a third sheet, finishing with the cheese. Do the same with the remaining 3 sheets of phyllo pastry so that you have 2 stacks of pastry. Using a 3-inch plain round cookie cutter, cut the phyllo layers into circles, and place them on a heavy baking sheet. Alternatively, divide the pastry into rectangular 4 x 1¼ inch wafers.

2 Bake in a preheated 350 degree oven, for 15 minutes until crisp and light brown. Remove from the baking sheet and cool on a wire rack.

Makes 20 round crackers or 36 rectangular ones

6 sheets phyllo pastry,
  12½ x 8½ inches, defrosted if frozen
6 tablespoons butter, melted
6 tablespoons finely grated
  Swiss cheese

piroshki

These are small crescent-shaped pastries traditionally served as an accompaniment to borscht and other Russian soups, but also excellent as a cocktail savory. They freeze very well in their raw state, to be defrosted and baked as required.

I tablespoon butter

I small onion, minced

2 garlic cloves, crushed

6 tablespoons very finely chopped
   mushrooms

½ cup cooked meat (chicken, beef,
   ham), very finely chopped or
   ground, or chopped mixed
   vegetables fried in a little butter
   until soft

I hard-boiled egg, very finely chopped

2 tablespoons minced parsley

2 tablespoons very finely chopped dill

I tablespoon lemon juice

beaten egg or milk, to glaze

salt and pepper

Pastry:

2 cups all-purpose flour

pinch of salt

½ cup butter or hard margarine

¼ cup shortening

I egg yolk

3 tablespoons sour cream

1 First prepare the pastry. Sift the flour and salt into a bowl. Cut the fats into small pieces and rub them into the flour until the mixture resembles fine bread crumbs. This can be done in a food processor, stopping and starting the machine to ensure that the pastry does not become over-processed. Mix the egg yolk with the sour cream, then sprinkle on to the crumbled pastry, and stir to make a dough. If you are using a food processor, pulse several times, just enough to make the dough hold together. Turn on to a lightly floured work surface, gather together into a ball and knead lightly. Cover and chill while making the filling.

2 Melt the butter in a skillet and gently fry the onion and garlic until soft but not colored. Stir in the mushrooms and fry until cooked and all the moisture has been driven off. Stir in the cooked meat or fried vegetables, the egg, parsley and dill. Season to taste with salt and pepper and add the lemon juice to sharpen. Set aside to cool.

3 Roll out the pastry very thinly — no more than about ¹⁄₁₆ inch thick on a lightly floured surface. Cut 2½ inch circles from the dough and place a little of the cold filling on one half of each circle. Brush the edge of the other half with beaten egg and fold the pastry over to enclose the filling. Press the edges together and crimp with the prongs of a fork. Place the piroshki on a lightly greased baking sheet. Brush with beaten egg or milk to glaze and bake in a preheated 425 degree oven for 5–8 minutes until golden.

Makes about 32

Jerusalem artichoke chips

These have a crisp exterior, yet are meltingly tender inside. They have a subtle flavor and make an excellent accompaniment for broiled or roast poultry and game. When thinly sliced, they can be served like potato chips and are good scattered over Jerusalem Artichoke Soup (page 124) or in a leafy salad.

1 Peel the artichokes and cut them into slices about 2 inches long and ½ inch wide, or cut them into thin slices as required. Rinse and dry the pieces carefully.

2 Heat the oil in a deep-fryer or large saucepan to 350–375 degrees, or until a cube of bread browns in 30 seconds. Deep-fry the artichoke pieces in small batches until tender, crisp and golden in color. Drain on paper towels, season generously and serve immediately.

Serves 4–6

CHEF'S TIP The chips or slices can be prepared in advance, cooked only until they are pale in color, then reheated in batches in hot oil at 400 degrees before serving.

1–1½ pounds (about 3 cups) large smooth Jerusalem artichokes

vegetable oil, for deep-frying

croûtons

Small cubes of bread fried in oil are frequently added to soup, vegetables, and salad dishes to add extra texture, flavor, and interest. For garlic or chili croûtons, infuse the oil with 2–3 crushed garlic cloves or 1 small chopped fresh chili for several hours before straining the oil and frying the bread. Nut-flavored oils can also be used.

**3 slices of white bread, about
¼ inch thick
4–5 tablespoons sunflower or olive oil**

1 Remove the crusts from the bread and cut the bread into ¼ inch cubes. The croûtons can be larger, depending on what they are to be served with. When used as a soup garnish, they are more elegant when small.

2 Heat the oil in a skillet and add the cubes of bread, tossing, and turning them to coat in the oil. Fry over a gentle heat until evenly colored and a light golden brown. Drain on paper towels and use as required. Croûtons can be stored in an airtight container for several weeks, or they can be frozen.

Makes 6 tablespoons croûtons, enough to serve 6

pickled cucumber

Pickling is an easy and tasty way to use up excess cucumbers. Pickles need to mature for several hours or overnight, so prepare in advance. It will keep well in the refrigerator for several weeks.

1 Combine all the ingredients in a non-metallic bowl, cover and leave to marinate for several hours. Pack into a sterilized jar, cover and refrigerate.

Makes 1¾ cups, enough to serve 4–6

**8 ounces cucumber, cut into little
   sticks, ¼ inch wide
6 tablespoons rice vinegar
2 tablespoons sweet cooking sake
   (mirin)
4 tablespoons cider vinegar
¼ teaspoon dried chili flakes
2 garlic cloves, chopped
½ teaspoon salt
2 teaspoons brown sugar
pinch of ground cloves
pinch of ground cinnamon
pepper**

polenta cakes

Polenta, also known as cornmeal or yellow meal, is ground maize. It is usually sunshine yellow in color, but there is also a white variety, and a beautiful dark purple one, a strain of Indian maize known as blue cornmeal. Whatever its color, polenta is an essential ingredient in the cooking of northern Italy, many parts of the U.S., and the West Indies. It has a sweet nutty taste and comes in varying degrees of coarseness, ranging from the most commonly used Italian golden polenta, which is coarse ground, to finely ground American cornmeal and West Indian ground maize, which may be coarse or fine. In Italy, polenta is traditionally used for making a thick mush with water, broth, or milk, which is eaten "wet" with lots of butter and Parmesan cheese. These broiled polenta cakes, made from cold polenta, are another traditional dish.

1 Melt the butter in a large saucepan and fry the onion until soft but not browned. Add the water and bring to a boil. Gradually pour in the polenta, stirring all the time, first with a wire whisk and then with a wooden spoon, so the polenta remains smooth and there are no lumps. Cook over a gentle heat for about 4–5 minutes, or follow the instructions on the packet. Stir in the Parmesan cheese and season with salt and pepper.

2 Lightly oil a 13 x 9 x ½ inch jellyroll pan. Line the pan with plastic wrap and oil it. Tip the prepared polenta into the pan and smooth the top. Cover with a piece of aluminum foil and leave until cool and set. This will take about 20 minutes, but the polenta can be made the day before, ready for cutting and broiling as required.

3 When the polenta is set, turn it out on to a board. Cut it into 6 squares, then 12 triangles. Brush a heavy cookie sheet with a little oil and set the polenta triangles on top. Brush each one with a little oil.

4 Cook the polenta triangles on a ridged cast iron grill pan or under a preheated broiler for about 3 minutes on each side. Serve hot.

Makes 12

4 tablespoons butter

I large onion, minced

I quart water

2 cups instant polenta or instant yellow cornmeal

4 tablespoons Parmesan cheese, freshly grated

2 tablespoons olive oil

salt and pepper

mung dhal

A rich lentil purée, quick and easy to prepare using lentils that do not need to be pre-soaked. Serve with any spicy vegetable stew, or with rice or Indian bread. Mung dhal also makes an excellent spread for crostini or crisp crackers. When mixed with finely chopped green onion (scallion), it makes a delicious sandwich filling.

1 Wash and drain the lentils. Put them in a large saucepan with the turmeric, chili powder, cinnamon, and vegetable broth. Stir to combine and bring to a boil. Reduce the heat immediately, cover and simmer gently for 20–40 minutes until the lentils are soft and the broth almost absorbed. The mixture should have a creamy consistency, but the lentils should retain some of their texture.

2 Heat the ghee or oil in a skillet and fry the onion and garlic until a light golden color. Stir in the cumin seeds and fry until they begin to splutter. Pour over the lentil mixture and stir to combine. Stir in the coriander, season with salt, and serve sprinkled with the garam masala.

Makes 1 pound 11 ounces (about 2¾ cups), enough to serve 4–6

I cup red lentils
½ teaspoon turmeric
½ teaspoon chili powder
I inch piece of cinnamon stick
3 cups hot vegetable broth or water
2–3 tablespoons ghee or sunflower oil
I large onion, thinly sliced
1–2 garlic cloves, crushed
½ teaspoon cumin seeds
I tablespoon finely chopped
  coriander (cilantro)
salt
¼ teaspoon garam masala, to serve

index

Author's Acknowledgements:

I am indebted to many people for their assistance on this book.

To the Professionals: To Laura Bamford for her confidence in the project; to Polly Manguel, for her patience and understanding; to Sasha Judelson for commissioning this book; to Jeni Wright, for her sensitive editing; to Katey Day, for always being there, particularly in the final pressured editing phase; to Sandra Lane, who has brought the text to life with her photography and to the designer, Geoff Fennell, who has fashioned a very beautiful and seductive book.

To Friends: To Owen and Ann Harry, for providing me with the most perfect writing house in which to be inspired and for supplying a variety of homegrown vegetables for my recipe tests; to Ronnie and Gwen Buchanan, for their constant support and friendship; to Maureen and Roy Haybeard, who, at short notice, included dishes from my experimenting on their meal table; to Alison Gray, for her kindness and patience in typing the finished work and deciphering my pencil jottings; and last but by no means least, to my constant companion and friend, Bruce, without whose love, support, and understanding this book would not have been written.

Photographic Acknowledgements:
Patrick McLeavey/Conran Octopus page 39

Notes

Eggs should be medium unless otherwise stated.

Milk should be whole milk unless otherwise stated.

Pepper should be freshly ground black pepper unless otherwise stated.

Fresh herbs should be used unless otherwise stated.

Ovens should be preheated to the specific temperature — if using a fan-assisted oven, follow the manufacturer's instructions for adjusting the time and temperature.